The Silver Birch Books

Teachings of Silver Birch   first published in 1938
Silver Birch Speaks   first published in 1949

The cassette, "Silver Birch Speaks," recorded at the Hannen Swaffer Home Circle, is available from the publishers, Psychic Press Limited.

Silver Birch books now out of print

More Teachings of Silver Birch   first published 1941
Wisdom of Silver Birch   first published 1944
More Wisdom of Silver Birch   first published 1945
Silver Birch Speaks Again   first published 1952
Philosophy of Silver Birch   first published 1969
Silver Birch Anthology   first published 1955
Guidance from Silver Birch   first published 1966
More Philosophy of Silver Birch   first published 1979

Light From Silver Birch

Compiled by Pam Riva,
the medium's secretary

Psychic Press Limited
20 Earlham Street
London, WC2H 9LW

This edition 1984

© Psychic Press Ltd

ISBN 0 85384 058 X

Reprinted by Photobooks (Bristol) Ltd
and bound by W. H. Ware Ltd, Clevedon

Contents

1: Light from Silver Birch

Why were you born? What will happen when you die? How can you live a happier, more fulfilling life?

Is there an intelligent Mind behind Creation, a plan for the universe, and for you?

These enigmas have been pondered by every thinker since the dawn of civilisation.

Now light is shed on such vital questions by one who lived in our world, and has progressed to a more spiritual realm.

Accepting a divine mission as torchbearer to dispel man's darkness, he found the means to communicate through an earthly instrument.

Soon a small band gathered to listen and learn. One, a respected Fleet Street journalist and critic, lent the group his name.

Three members of the Hannen Swaffer Home Circle were of Jewish origin. Three were Gentiles. But the communicator, adopting the name Silver Birch, told them, "our allegiance is not to a Creed, not to a Book, not to a Church, but to the Great Spirit of Life and to His eternal natural laws."

One man, whether he be a Jesus or a Hitler, can change the course of human destiny.

The two-world partnership of Maurice Barbanell and the wise, unseen communicator who spoke through his entranced physical body has changed the course of countless lives,

1

*bringing comfort to mourners and hope to the despairing,
winning friends all over the world.*

★   ★   ★

Who is Silver Birch?

*Certainly his future medium, an 18-year-old Atheist scepti-
cally attending a London home circle in 1920, did not know.
And if he knew 61 years later, he did not tell.*

*Yet he devoted the intervening years to spreading through-
out the world the words spoken by his guide and mentor. His
self-imposed task was pursued tirelessly, faithfully, to the last
day of his earthly life.*

*In this volume are gathered the final teachings transmitted
before the medium joined his mentor in the Larger Life.*

*This collection is dedicated to three spiritual pilgrims; the
medium, who developed into a respected editor, journalist,
author and businessman; Silver Birch's first earthly friend,
Sylvia, the medium's devoted wife for 49 years, an author,
poetess and animal welfare worker; and Frances Moore, the
home circle member whose impeccable shorthand recorded the
spirit guide's words.*

Throughout this volume, Silver Birch's words are
printed in roman type. The only other text in this
typeface is the chapter titled, "Maurice Barbanell's own
story," written by the medium before his passing in
July, 1981.

*In italics are comments and questions from circle members
and visitors.*

PAM RIVA

2: Silver Birch's Message to Humankind

We are engaged in a massive task all over your world where so many areas are engulfed in almost unique darkness.

We have to labour so as to ensure that the light of the spirit will break through that murk and enable people to have access to the source of all life, the supreme power that can enrich them physically, mentally and spiritually. This is the sublime task that activates all we are trying to do.

Our progress is slow. The difficulties that have to be overcome are massive, but gradually we are breaking through. We are establishing bridgeheads in new areas. The power of the spirit is here to stay in your world. It will bring its benign influence to bear on millions.

I and others in my world and yours are privileged to serve in this field of noble labour. Therefore we have the responsibility always of ensuring that we do nothing that in any way would mar the trust that is reposed in us. You have access to the power of the spirit that can reach you. So have I, and when necessary I can call upon it for added strength to help you to serve others just as we try to serve you.

Because of our knowledge, we are imbued with

optimism and hope, knowing that at all times the power that is behind us is greater than any that can be mustered in your world. There is no need for defeatism, or for depression. All goes according to the divine plan and will continue to do so. Man can hinder, man can delay; but man cannot destroy the plan that the supreme power has originated to help your world.

We are privileged because our knowledge has enabled us to see beyond the confines of matter and to have glimpses of the larger, beauteous life in a world which is superior to anything that earth can offer. We are aware of higher, evolved beings in this world whose one desire is to help, inspire and utilise earthly instruments as channels for a divine power that can bring a rich beneficence in its train.

It can heal the sick, comfort the mourner, guide those who have lost the way, replace ignorance with knowledge, darkness with light, give strength to the weary, drink to the thirsty and provide guidelines for those who wish to fulfil themselves according to the divine plan.

No prayer for help is unheard; no desire to serve does not get a response. The whole emphasis from our world is to uplift all who are ready to utilise their gifts in the service of those less fortunate than themselves.

Always there is accessible to us not only inspiration and revelation, but the power of the spirit which brings in its train magnificent benefits to be freely bestowed on all who are ready to receive them.

It is our bounden duty so to evolve, develop and unfold that we manifest a greater divinity as time goes on.

Life is deathless; the grave has no power to end life. Love is deathless, because love is stronger than death. Life and love are the twin integral powers of the Great Spirit which we all possess and which we can use as we develop and unfold them, together with any gifts with which we have been endowed, to serve those who are less fortunate than ourselves.

There are more worshippers of mammon than there are of the Great Spirit.

Those who should be the spiritual masters, with knowledge of all that the spirit has to enrich human life, are ignorant because they are bound and restricted by believing in creeds, doctrines and dogmas that did not originate with the Great Spirit but with human beings in your world. Those who should have vision are, alas, among the blind ones.

For that reason there is much work to be done for the power of the spirit to make itself felt, to give the evidence that life and love are eternal, to allow that power of the spirit to show its beneficence by healing the sick, even when some of the best doctors in your world had said no more can be done.

Moreover this tremendous power of the spirit, because it is divine, can sustain, direct, give guidance when seemingly all else has failed. It can point the way so that individuals can live to the fullest extent of their nature physically, mentally and spiritually, realising the purpose earthly life has in the universal scheme, and thus fulfil themselves as the natural law intends they should so that their temporary sojourn on earth should enable them to be prepared for the greater life that is inevitable for everyone in your world.

There is no need for fear or anxiety as to what the future will hold for you. Spirit is stronger than matter. The Great Spirit is stronger than any human individual. The plan of the Great Spirit will ultimately prevail.

You all have your parts to play. You could all do something to make the place where you live brighter, richer because you are dwelling there. The way will be shown when you are spiritually ready to receive direction.

Be full of cheer, have faith and hope, because you know that once you have made your contact with the greatest power in the universe you will not be failed. Always there will come to your aid those who love you, not only because they are related to you, but others who desire to use you to serve, so that the frontiers of knowledge may be extended wider and further throughout the whole of the world.

My message always is, lift up your hearts and do not despair. Every day is the dawn of opportunities, not only for self-fulfilment, but providing the means where you can help others who will be brought to you so that your purpose and theirs in your world will be fulfilled.

★   ★   ★

We pray that we shall play our part in helping the eternal processes of creation, to drive out the darkness, the ignorance, the superstition, the selfishness, the violence and all that are hideous cancers in your world.

Our task is to replace them with a sublime knowledge that will enable the children of the Great Spirit to fill themselves with the radiance that could be theirs.

In expressing our gratitude for all that we have received, we pray that we may be worthy to continue to be channels for this divine wisdom and power, thus being able to serve others less fortunate than ourselves and so help to strengthen and widen the spheres of influence that can teach an increasing number of people how to fulfil themselves.

This is the prayer of Thy Indian servant who seeks always to serve.

3: Why Were you Born?

What is the reason for earthly life?

Are we freak effects of natural causes? Or has a Master Architect designed a plan for His creations?

Is there a blueprint for each one of us to seek out, unfold and build, be it falsely or truly?

★ ★ ★

The object of all earthly existence is that the human spirit is to be quickened.

Earthly life has a purpose for all who dwell on your planet. It is sad that there are millions who are unaware of the spiritual reality on which their lives are based. Like troglodytes they live in a spiritual gloom that is almost a vacuum.

Their perspective is wrong; their focus is wrong; their vision is wrong. They have no idea of the vast richness that life has to offer them. Once you are aware of spiritual truths you are transformed because you know what it is you must achieve.

We are all human beings. Thus we have the flaws of imperfection within us. If we were perfect, we would not be in your world or in ours. We would have joined the Great Spirit, the only perfect power in the universe.

We recognise the frailties of human nature. But you must regard every problem as a challenge not only to be met and accepted, but to be overcome so that the indwelling spirit, as a result, is more fortified, grows, develops, unfolds, and you emerge stronger.

It is not possible for you who dwell in earthly surroundings not to be confronted with heights and depths and the ups and downs of the varying circumstances which pertain to your world.

It is why you are placed there so that you can, because of the variety of circumstance, enable your spirit, the eternal you, to be able to express latent qualities that can be manifested only when confronted with difficulty and adversity.

It is not when the sun shines that the soul finds itself. It is not in a bed of roses that the soul comes into its own. It is in the hazards and challenges, the difficulties, the hurdles and the obstacles. These provide the only means by which the soul can realise its latent divinity.

This is the story of every pilgrim on the road to spiritual knowledge. There have to be heartbreak, sorrow and suffering to appreciate fully the compensations that will follow. The individuals who will give service must be tried and tested, sometimes to their uttermost strength.

There is a plan for every child of the Great Spirit. There are no accidents, no chances, no coincidences. Everything operates according to natural law which knows nothing of miracles or necessity for intervention. The natural law is perfect because it is conceived by perfect mind.

There are no exceptions to the natural law, which makes provision for all that exists, not only in the universe but even in the immeasurable cosmos. Wherever you look, the natural law operates. Nothing is too small to be ignored, and nothing too large to be outside the framework of how the natural law operates. And it operates for you, as it does for me and for everybody.

So you know that action and reaction are equal and opposite. You know that you have to plumb the depths before you reach the heights. And you know that you have plumbed the depths, but have not reached the heights. That is why you have doubts about surviving.

But you will survive. I do not mean permanently in your world, because immortality is not part of earthly existence. Everything material has a period placed on it when it must finish its task. It must dissolve, disintegrate and be resolved into the original constituents that made its existence possible.

Your body will follow that pattern as part of a preordained course, but you will survive because you have no alternative, because surviving is part of the natural law.

In some religions they teach that there is survival for those who believe in certain doctrines and creeds. But survival has nothing to do with religion or with human beliefs, aspirations and hopes. Survival is an inflexible law, automatic in its operation.

You will survive because the spirit comes to earth to develop, to grow, to unfold and to prepare itself for its real home, not the transitory abode which earth provides. You will come home where you began, and continue to live after having left what earth has to offer, so that you can play your part in the great universal scheme.

Every child of the Great Spirit has a part to play in the infinite scheme. There will be difficulties, but these are the challenges that have to be met, accepted and triumphed over. Handicaps and obstacles are all part of the necessary preparation for an evolving, developing spiritual nature.

Yours is a very dense, material world where the vibrations are heavy, slow, sluggish, ponderous. The vibrations of the spirit are delicate, sensitive, subtle, and to be expressed there has to be a catalyst for the individual.

You will not find spiritual truths when the sun is shining, if you are surrounded by riches, and wealth and possessions. You will not find spiritual truths when you have no problems. The catalyst will work only when you are in trouble.

A storm can often do more to help you to unfold spiritually than the sun. It is in the fire that the steel is forged. It is in the crushing process that the gold is refined and purified to emerge in all its glistening colour. And it is similarly for the human spirit to be tried and tested again and again, before it can emerge with a greater divinity being expressed than had happened before.

The gold is there, but the ore has to be crushed before the purity of the metal can be made visible. The steel has to be forged in the crucible of fire. And so it is with all of you.

You would not be interested in the things of the spirit, which are your eternal possessions, the only enduring and abiding realities, until you are ready to receive them. So you have to be tried and tested, just as the steel has to be tried and tested.

You have to suffer. You have to endure privation,

perhaps ill-health, some crisis that will touch your soul, that spark of the divine, and begin to fan it into a beauteous flame. There is no other way. It is only in the darkness that you will find the light, only in ignorance that you will gain knowledge. Life must be a polarity, or if you like a duality, in which it is said action and reaction are equal and opposite.

The soul cannot come into its own until it is touched. This usually means when it seems to the individual there is no hope in his world, no light, no guidance to be found. The abyss of despair has been reached, the fear that he or she will be plunged into the depths and not recover. It is at that moment that the soul can be awakened.

Thus we in our world have to wait patiently until your soul is ready. You say in your world that you may lead a horse to water, but you cannot make it drink. You have to be ready.

I have had a longer experience than all of you. It gives me a greater appreciation of the perfection of the natural laws that encompass us all and ensure that provision is made for everyone.

I am puzzled sometimes when I visit my friends on earth who have knowledge, and I see them worried and anxious. The knowledge is their foundation which should assure them that no harm or injury can befall their eternal spirit. Those with knowledge should be living in the light and never fear what the morrow will bring.

There is nothing in your world that you need worry about. You have within you the armoury of the spirit, the divine potential which you can utilise to help in any emergency or crisis that comes your way. There is no problem you cannot solve by calling on the power that is within you and by appealing to the power that is without.

4: *Your Path to Fulfilment*

How can you live a happier, more fulfilling life?
Silver Birch lights the way of eternal progress with this
advice.

★ ★ ★

We are all the channels of the Great Spirit. It is a privilege to serve. There is no religion higher than service. Service is the true coin of the spirit. It is noble to serve.

To serve is to enrich the lives of others and your own. To serve is to bring comfort to those who think there is nothing left for them in your world.

It is in service that we find inner peace, tranquillity and repose. It is in service that we obtain steadfastness that enables us to have complete confidence in the overruling power, to strive to get closer and closer to the Great Spirit

The summit of all attainment is the Great White Spirit, the infinite power of love and wisdom that has devised the boundless universe in which we live and has brought into being natural laws which ensure that everything and everybody come within their framework.

Nothing exists apart from the Great Spirit, therefore the Great Spirit is all. The Great Spirit is responsible for every phase of life in whatever aspect it manifests, large or small, complex or simple. It exists because spirit has given it motivation. You cannot separate yourself from the Great Spirit because the Great Spirit is immanent in all creation. Whatever people may say, it cannot alter the fact that the Great Spirit is in all, the Great Spirit is all and all is the Great Spirit.

Nobody and nothing is higher than the Great White Spirit, the infinite creator, the supreme arbiter whose love and wisdom are responsible for the majestic universe and whose perfect intelligence devised all the natural laws which encompass every manifestation of being, majestically mighty or microscopically minute, and has made provision for all and everything that exists. So perfect is the operation of these natural laws that nothing and nobody can be outside their scope.

Nothing and nobody can be too small, be neglected, overlooked or forgotten by that supreme power which has ensured that everyone has access to the divine fount.

This is because a portion of the Great Spirit is within everybody and everything that moves and lives and has its being.

We exist because the Great Spirit has breathed into each one of us a portion of divinity, and that is the link that binds us to the Great Spirit and to one another.

There is no power on earth or in the world beyond that can sever that link, and because of it we have access to the infinite storehouse of wisdom, truth and revelation.

The power of life, the spirit, is in all and everybody. It is to be seen at its highest in the vast human family, all of whom contain a portion of divinity that links them for eternity not only to the Great Spirit but to one another. This link is part of an unbreakable chain.

We, with longer experience than all of you, never cease to wonder at the divine wisdom which has devised the entire scheme of boundless life.

We express our gratitude for the constant flow of truth, wisdom and inspiration that always extend the boundaries of our minds and give an increasing awareness of who and what we truly are, the power that resides within each one of us, the gifts which have been bestowed on us that we should utilise them in the service of those who are unaware of the richness of the spirit that could be theirs, our relationship to one another and to the Great Spirit.

The natural laws have so arranged it that at all times we are united with the divine architect who breathed life into each one of us, and thus created a bond that nothing on earth or in the worlds beyond can ever break.

The power of love guides and directs the sublime scheme to ensure that for all time there will be harmony and the means available for all who are ready to receive the influx of power, wisdom, truth and inspiration.

Moreover we can each be the instruments of that sublime power that streams from the source of all being and brings in its train that tremendous beneficence that enriches all human life in your world, enables the sick to be healed, mourners to be comforted, the weary to obtain strength and guidance given to those who have lost their way.

We are all gifted with talents which we can develop to be used in the service of those unfortunates who do not share the priceless knowledge we have obtained. Our task is to become even better instruments through whom this majestic, divine power can flow and bring in its train all the benefits that are freely offered to those capable of receiving them.

★ ★ ★

Let me explain to you how the things of the spirit work. People in your world talk about the mystery of suffering, the purpose of illness, the reason for crises, difficulties and obstacles. These are the challenges that the human soul must encounter because they provide first the catharsis and then the catalyst that will enable them to appreciate spiritual truth.

As low as any soul can sink so correspondingly can it rise. That is the law of polarity, the law which says action and reaction are equal and opposite.

Hate and love, light and dark, storm and peace, these are opposite sides of the same coin.

I have my favourite saying. It says in your Bible, "Add to your faith knowledge." I say, "When you have knowledge, add faith to it." You cannot have all knowledge. You are human, restricted in your capacity, for your reception is of necessity limited.

The foundation of knowledge should be your base to enable you to withstand all the storms and tempests of earthly life, to be unshaken no matter what happens. Let your faith help you where your knowledge cannot take you.

We pride ourselves that when we come back we will win you by love and reason. We will not dictate to you. We will not ask you to do certain things. You will do them of your own free will. If anything we say from our life cannot pass the bar of your reason and makes it revolt, if it insults your intelligence, reject it.

We have to appeal not to the lowest, but to the highest within you, so that you will give your co-operation and allegiance because you desire to do so. You will find that you will be helped in your own sphere of activity, in your daily work. And you will reach other conditions where you can render service.

I hope I can render some service to you. You may not realise it, but you are being led along a pathway that could ultimately bring you a mental and spiritual richness that you have not so far enjoyed. I appreciate the problems that arise in your minds and the questions that inevitably you want to ask, but let me say that the only abiding reality in the whole universe is the spirit.

Matter by its very nature is ephemeral, transient. It has no permanence in the form that is physically manifested. Anything material exists only because it is given life by the spirit. It is the spirit which is the dynamic, the vivifying power that enables you and everybody else in your world to live. When the spirit withdraws, matter crumbles. Your body returns to the dust, but you, the spirit, continue on your eternal path of progress.

You are not bodies with spirits; you are spirits with bodies. The real you is not the countenance you behold in a mirror. That is only part of a physical apparatus, a complex machinery, that the spirit has to use to express itself in your world. Spirit is superior to matter; spirit is the king, matter is the servant.

You will find if you pursue this quest that your perspective and focus will change. You will begin to understand why you are on earth, what it is you have to achieve to fulfil your true self. If you are endowed with any gift, no matter what its form, you should develop it so that others can be served and enlightened.

You have to remember that you are imperfect beings living in an imperfect world. If the Great Spirit wanted you to be perfect you would not have been placed on earth. You have the choice, the free will, as to how you utilise the gifts, the powers, the talents with which you are endowed.

The essence of life on earth is it offers stark contrasts and polarities. It provides goodness and the lack of goodness. This does not obtain in our world, where each sphere does not have this contrast.

The object of earthly life is to make available a variety of experiences, to enable the soul to exercise its divine potential and emerge stronger as a result. And so you will have crimes, sin and violence.

Evolution is not in a straight line. It is in a spiral. At the top, things look beautiful; at the bottom they don't look so beautiful.

When I speak of spheres I do not necessarily mean round worlds. I mean planes of being, each graduating into the other, not separated geographically, from the lowest to the highest. It is an infinite evolution.

There is no summit to be attained. As the spirit unfolds, so it is realised there is more to be achieved. It is like knowledge. The more you have, the more you realise there is further knowledge to be gained.

The sphere or plane on which you exist in our world contains individuals at the same stage of spiritual development as you are. You can't go higher spiritually until you are ready. You can go lower, as many of us do in order to perform missionary work among the unenlightened beings in the lower spheres.

Progress consists in shedding imperfections and striving and growing towards perfection all the time.

Just live for the day. Greet each morning as the herald giving untold possibilities for character building that will enable you to fulfil yourselves and give life its purposefulness which, alas, is absent for too many in your world.

Strive to make the will of the Great Spirit your will, to be in tune with the divine power, to feel the arms of love around each one of you, to know that the mantle of protection is on your shoulders, to have no fear what the morrow will bring. Rejoice at the opportunities of service that are provided for you.

We are engaged in a great war. There have been many skirmishes and battles. The foes we fight are greed, envy, selfishness, by-products of the materialism that inflicts your world.

We demonstrate the divine power of the spirit that emanates from the source of all being, the infinite creator. We demonstrate that death is a door which opens to reveal the wondrous life of the realms of the spirit.

That is the war in which you are playing your part. The officers and generals have to be tried and tested to ensure that they will not fail at their posts when the thunder roars, the lightning flashes and the storm howls.

You will be shown the way by the many who love you from our world, not only those with whom you have a tie of blood, but others, because there is a kinship of mind and spirit. They can use you to serve the others who are less fortunate than we are.

We are all fellow travellers on the same spiritual pathway, which has many roads to take us towards the Great Spirit. Let us be grateful for any knowledge that has extended the boundaries of our minds and given us a greater understanding of the universe in which we dwell.

Knowledge brings responsibility; a price must be paid for it. If you have knowledge you are more responsible than those who are ignorant. We in our world will not fail those who co-operate with us in giving service. I wish it could be said that none in your world ever fails us, but, alas, it cannot be.

You are all helped more than you can realise. When ultimately you come to our world and assess all the results of what has been achieved, you will be surprised. We are touching souls; that is very important.

Consider the pitiful mess that others have made: the religions that have failed to fulfil their purpose, the misdirected scientists who do not realise the damage they can do, the philosophers in a morass of materialism that helps nobody, not even themselves. We are privileged to be the instruments of the Great Spirit, charged with a task that is important, and aware of the trust that is reposed in every one of us.

We will guide, we will encourage, we will strengthen, we will help, we will always urge you to serve, so that those who are brought to you will have their opportunity of gaining sublime truths which bring freedom to the spirit, mind and body and enable them to fulfil themselves, for that is the object of all earthly existence. You cannot measure what you can accomplish because there are no instruments that can measure the progress of the spirit.

If you enable one mourner to be comforted, one sick person to be healed, one individual to fulfil himself or herself, then the whole of your earthly life will not have been in vain. We are concerned with service, the coin of the spirit.

Do not allow dismay or fear to effect a lodgment within your being. Fear is the child of ignorance; knowledge should always drive out fear. You have access to the mightiest power in the universe. It is more majestic than any power known in your physical world. It is the supreme power. You can allow it to stream through you and perform its beneficent work.

Never allow yourself to become despondent or pessimistic. Those who are privileged to have the knowledge of fundamental, abiding spiritual realities should realise that no matter what are the prevailing circumstances, the spirit is stronger than matter. The solution can be found, though sometimes it means you have to wait for a little while before it can reach you.

It is our privilege to serve those less fortunate than ourselves. As we serve, so we are served by higher, evolved and enlightened beings who desire nothing for themselves but to inspire us to labour to spread light wherever there is darkness, truth where there is ignorance and help where it may be needed.

We welcome into our midst the many enfranchised and liberated beings whose one desire is to serve humanity by driving out the ignorance and superstition that prevent them from living the fullness of radiant life.

Let us try to be increasingly aware of the mighty powers that are around and about us, of the evolved beings who strive to use us as their instruments in the service of many who do not realise what they can achieve to fulfil themselves.

We are grateful for the fact that the supreme power of the spirit is able to flow through an increasing number of human earthly channels, spreading its beneficence and comforting mourners, healing the sick, guiding those who have lost their way and think there is no way for them to find the answers to their problems.

Wherever it effects a lodgment, a bridgehead becomes established and consolidated. Then it seeks another bridgehead to be established and consolidated. Thus gradually the power of the spirit will girdle your globe and be accessible to many more with the vast boons it has to offer.

We pray that as we have received so much from the source of all being – many have been enriched by its inspiration, wisdom and truth – that it may fortify and strengthen our resolve to help those less fortunate than ourselves, so that they can share in the richness and beauty, glory and radiance that the acquisition of this priceless knowledge brings.

Let us always be aware of the responsibility that knowledge brings. We cannot plead ignorance, because we have a truth that brings us mental and spiritual freedom. Let us pray for increasing opportunities for service, that we may find a better and closer harmony with the overruling power that instilled part of its divinity into each one of us.

Thus we will have an inner peace, a tranquillity, an awareness, a serenity that all is divinely well, and we have our parts to play in helping the infinite process of creation to be fulfilled.

★ ★ ★

"How is it that to find the spiritual we have to awaken? You tell us all human beings are linked in the spirit, yet so many people seem to miss it. I find this a mystery."

It is not such a seeming mystery as would appear on the surface. You must recognise that all of you are spirits with bodies, not even bodies with spirits. Matter exists because it is animated by the spirit, which is the spark of the divine embedded within every being and within everything that expresses life, no matter what form it takes.

Obviously the purpose of earthly incarnation is for the individual to have those experiences which will enable the soul to grow, unfold and develop, and to achieve that kind of progress that fits it for the next stage of life beyond the death of the body.

Your earth is the kindergarten, our world is the adult school. You are here to learn the lessons wisely and well, to educate the mind, to train the spirit to develop any gifts with which you have been divinely endowed, so that they can be utilised in the service of others in healing and in other ways.

"Is the ideal to train ourselves away from earthly things towards spiritual ones? Or should we gain all the earthly experiences we can?"

You must not divorce matter from spirit and suggest that these are watertight compartments that are in no way related. They are inter-related. While you are on earth, spirit controls matter, but matter regulates the extent of spirit control. You cannot isolate matter from spirit.

The whole object of earthly life is to have a variety of experiences that will fit the spirit for the next stage beyond earth when you have to pass into our world. That is why you come to earth in the first place. Earth is the training ground, the school where the spirit learns its lessons which will provide its equipment for the life beyond earth.

For that reason I say to you again and again that what you regard as the bad experiences can be the best ones for you. It is not in the sunshine that the soul finds itself, but in the storm. It is when the thunder rages and the lightning flashes.

You must be sharpened, purged, refined. You must experience the heights and depths. You must have the variety of experiences that earth provides for you. In this way the spirit emerges stronger, fortified, ready for what awaits it when death comes.

★ ★ ★

A young Vietnamese guest asked: "I would like to help in my spare time, but I don't know what to do. Can you guide me?"

Materially and spiritually you have travelled a long way. The fact that you are sitting where you are now is evidence that the power of the spirit was able to guide you at a time when it seemed no help was possible.

When there is the desire to serve, the opportunities will be provided, but do not be in a hurry. The criticism I have to make of many people in your world is that once they become aware of spiritual realities, and that has taken a long time, they are anxious to unfold whatever gifts they possess.

The way will be shown. Pray for guidance.

Life has given you many blows which almost destroyed your faith in human nature. Put not your trust altogether in people in your world. There is always the Great Spirit, the acme of love, wisdom, truth and knowledge.

When there is any doubt, withdraw into the silence where the strident noise of the physical world is stilled and your spirit can find more expression. Then as you attune yourself you will find there comes an inner peace, tranquillity, repose, and resolution that will enable you to be sure that what is best for you will be revealed.

That is the only way I can answer your question. You are in very good hands; you will not be left alone. You will find as the days unfold they will bring you many opportunities to serve others.

★ ★ ★

Another visitor said: "After receiving healing I started with a group to give healing. Then I branched out in a different direction, helping people wherever I could. Does it make any difference which way you serve as long as you are doing something worth while?"

How would you answer?

"I feel that spiritually the answer is 'yes.' I am doing all I possibly can. But sometimes when I see mountains of trouble I wonder if I have done something to upset the spirit world."

Service is the coin of the spirit. There is no religion higher than service. It is noble to serve. If you cannot serve where you would like, then serve wherever the opportunity comes. When the door opens you go through it. Never bang on a closed door; it is a waste of time and energy.

Do not be upset too much by difficulties. Difficulties

are challenges. If you had no difficulties, problems, obstacles or hindrances, there would be no opportunities for your latent powers to express themselves.

In moments of crisis you become aware that you have an inner reservoir of strength on which you can call. Usually you scratch only the surface of what you can get. There is no difficulty so great that you have not the power, with the inner strength you possess and the guidance you can receive, to triumph over it.

We have to work in your world, and are aware of its limitations. We are aware that the channels we use are human, sometimes fragile and wayward. But we have to do the best with the material we have.

I always tell people who come here that whenever they have any doubt, they should cast their mind back to the time when they had reached what they thought was the uttermost depths. It was a pit from which they thought they could never be rescued. Yet when it happened to you the way was shown. It will continue to be shown.

You are expected to do the best you can. You are not perfect. You will not attain perfection in your world, or in ours; it is an endless process.

My friends here have heard me say it many times. When you fall down you can always pick yourself up.

The guest told Sylvia Barbanell:

"I have had a great deal of help from your book, 'When a Child Dies,' since I 'lost' two daughters.

"I have just heard of someone who has lost a little boy. When I pass it on to her I hope it will give her as much satisfaction as I received when reading it."

The leaven does work, and it will continue to do so.

We are on the winning side in this tremendous battle being fought. We will emerge as the victors, not the losers. The power behind us is the greatest in the cosmos. It is the power of the Great Spirit, mightier than any force known in your world. I rest my confidence in that power because of the wonders I have seen it perform. I see no cause for worry.

He advised a medium:

Keep trying; do not give in. Despair is not good for you. It produces blackness, in which help cannot shed its light. I am optimistic always, because I have had the privilege of seeing the sublimity of how the natural laws work. I know they will fulfil themselves.

Man can hinder and delay. But he cannot prevent the power of the spirit from increasing its beneficence in your world, finding new bridgeheads, consolidating them, building lighthouses of the spirit to shed their rays and guide travellers out of the darkness of their sorrow into the illumination we offer. Do not be afraid of the challenges that come your way. Accept them, and know that the power of the spirit will enable you to triumph as a result.

"I have doubts sometimes whether I will be able to live up to what is expected of me. We spend our lives reassuring people, yet we doubt sometimes."

Your name is not Thomas, you should not doubt. Blessed are they who have seen and heard. Theirs is the great privilege of having insight and glimpses into the wondrous life that is around and about them. It is filled with beings whose desire is only to serve, who want nothing for themselves, but seek to help people who feel helpless. That is the task on which we are all engaged.

I am aware of human fallibility, of its doubts and fears. But you will learn gradually that when you place your complete confidence in that power which has revealed its glories, beauties, radiance, strength and guidance, it will not fail. It can be said that many have failed us. It cannot be said that we have failed them.

I repeat that you cannot measure what you are doing. You are helping souls to find themselves when they did not think it was possible.

How sad it is to behold millions who are unaware of who and what they are, blind and deaf to spiritual realities. They have lost their way and live in a morass, floundering all the time because they cannot tread paths of certainty.

Because of what we know let us be aware of our responsibility to be available to serve those who come to us, to offer them light in their darkness.

5: What Is Death?

Death is the sloughing off of the physical body as the spirit body gradually emerges.

There is nothing to fear in death. Death is the great liberator; death brings freedom.

You rejoice when babies come into your world. There are many who cry in our world when babies are about to be born into your world.

Similarly there is weeping when people die in your world, but there is rejoicing in ours. Death means that the life has served its purpose, or should have done, and the individual is ready to enjoy all the tremendous richness and beauty that the spirit life has to offer.

You have the spirit, which is the divine essence that enables you to live. You have a physical body that exists because it is animated by the spirit. When the spirit finally withdraws – I stress finally because temporarily it does so when you sleep, but returns when you wake – death comes to the physical body because the animation has gone.

Those who have clairvoyance will see that the parting is finally accomplished when the cord connecting the spirit body to the physical one, after being extended as the spirit body gradually moves away, is cut. When that severance takes place, death occurs. There is nothing and nobody in your world who can by any means enable the physical body to live again.

* ★ ★

"A problem has arisen because of new techniques of removing organs. Now doctors wait for people to die to take a heart or kidneys. The question is: 'Is the person dead? Am I at liberty to take the organ?'"

I know about transplants, and am aware that the motive is often a very good one. But I must say that I am opposed to transplanting any part of the human body to other people.

"Some people believe it is necessary to leave the body in a state of peace for a given amount of time. This is because of the present-day tendency to whisk people into laboratories and open them up for experimental purposes. Do you think this is in any way harmful to the soul or the spirit?"

It depends on whether the individual has any knowledge of spiritual matters. If there is ignorance, there can be temporary harm to the soul. Even when the cord connecting the physical and spirit bodies is cut, there is still a certain amount of interplay due to the long association of the two forms of being.

Generally it is considered advisable, where there is complete ignorance of spiritual truths, for an interval of three days to elapse before there is either burial or cremation.

What happens after than is unimportant. If people wish to give their bodies to help knowledge for purposes which can be of service to others that is a matter for them to decide. But let me also say this. There is a time to be born and there is a time to die. If that time to die is reached then transplants will not succeed in maintaining you in your world.

"But there is a problem of people on a plane which crashes and they die instantly. What is the effect on them?"

Exactly the same as I have said. Those who have knowledge of spiritual realities will not be affected. Those who have not will be affected because of the shock. But in the process of time, awareness and realisation will come.

"An accidental death predisposes one to accept reincarnation."

I am not happy about the use of the word "accident" because I know only of cause and effect in operation. Whatever you regard as accidental can be due only to the operation of the law of cause and effect. As to the question of reincarnation, that is a more complex matter.

★ ★ ★

"I have been watching on TV 'The Making of Mankind.' It set me thinking about the origin of the human soul. In the very early beginning does the human soul emerge from a group of an animal species?"

No.

"Does that mean the animal kingdom is separated from us?"

No.

"How does the human soul first emerge?"

It does not emerge at all. It has no beginnings.

"I always thought that the human soul has gradually evolved."

No, the body has evolved. The soul is part of the Great Spirit which always was and always will be.

The soul has always been. It is individuated when it becomes incarnated into the human frame. The soul has no beginning and no end. It says in your Bible, "Before

Abraham was I am." The spirit has always existed; the spirit was not created out of nothing.

Spirit is life. Life is universal. Souls, like spirits, do not have beginnings and ends. Spirit individuates when it incarnates into human form but as spirit or soul it has always existed.

★ ★ ★

"I would like to know about the eternity of the soul. One speaks of old and younger souls. Is the soul always so, or is it created? From where do we come? Are all souls reincarnated ones, or are there some new from the Great Spirit?"

Souls are not created; they have always existed.

I quoted your Bible: in the words of the Nazarene, "Before Abraham was I am." As spirit you have always existed. Spirit did not have to be created. There never was any stage when nothing became something.

Spirit, the dynamic, the essence, the vitality that is life, has always existed. Spirit is the energy out of which every manifestation of life is formed, whether it be a plant, a bird, a tree, an animal, a human. Spirit is the mainspring of existence.

When a child is conceived it is not a new soul or a new spirit. It is part of the eternal spirit that has always been in existence.

It becomes individualised and that individuality functions for a short time.

But the soul can have many facets. Some of these facets can reincarnate in your world and bring added lustre to the diamond of the soul. There are old and young souls. You do not manufacture new souls by conception. You provide them with a physical body to express themselves.

When birth is to be achieved and a physical body prepared for its existence, spirit becomes individuated and incarnates into your world. There is nothing new in that spirit. It is taking individual form. It is becoming a person. When he or she is developed and leaves your world, it is a facet of a larger diamond to which it adds its contribution.

"If there is a time for everybody to be born, equally there is a time for them to die. What happens when there is a Caesarian operation; somebody steps in and alters the time of birth?"

It alters only the time of entry into your world. It does not alter the time when the spirit has started at the moment of conception to begin to express itself. There is also the free will where an individual can decide to end his physical life, but then automatically he or she is confronted with the law of retribution.

"When a child is to be born it often happens that the doctors accelerate the birth with artificial means. A baby is born earlier than it is due. Does this have any influence astrologically?"

The things that worry you! The only vital fact about entry into your world is when life first begins to show itself. That is when conception takes place, not when a baby is born. I am not interested in the astrological arguments. With conception, earth life begins. Without conception there is no earthly life.

"The Pope in Brazil complained about the poorness of the people and stressed at the same time that family planning should never be allowed. How does this make sense?"

The Pope is a very good man, but he is not the repository of all the knowledge that exists in the universe. Family planning will continue in your world because it

is your responsibility. But if a child is to be born, it will
be born despite all family planning.

* * *

*"I know some people who genuinely do not wish to survive
death. What would you say to them?"*

I know some people who genuinely do not wish to be
born into your world. They can do nothing about it.
You cannot opt out of the natural law. It will operate
irrespective of what you think about it. You see in the
unfolding processes of nature how this panorama presents itself unceasingly, irrespective of man's desires,
wishes, or even objections.

*"Are we then forced to come into this world if we do not
wish to do so? I always thought this is our choice."*

This is not always the case. There is a choice in our
world as there is a choice in yours. When the soul
knows it has work to do, it will incarnate into your
world. There are some who have no desire to do so, but
they come because they have work to do, or they have a
karmic condition to fulfil.

*"Could it ever be true it is sometimes planned that a person
will commit suicide?"*

No! The planning is done by the soul before it
incarnates.

"Are there no lessons one can learn by commiting suicide?"

No! The Great Spirit gives life. It is not your responsibility to shorten it.

"When a person passes, does he know he has died?"

Not all. The majority do, but it takes some time for a
complete awareness to be realised.

"Do spirit people not help?"

Yes, we always help, even if the one who is being

transferred from your world may be unaware of the aid he is receiving.

All is known by the powers that be. There is a hierarchy of evolved beings, some of whom have never incarnated in your world. They are charged with fulfilling the divine plan. It is an overall one, and encompasses everything and everybody. There is nothing that can be outside the scope of universal natural law.

"When people die, relatives and loved ones meet them and help them over. Does it mean they are all at the same level?"

No, because those who love you will in most cases have evolved spiritually since their passing. They will come down, as it were, so as to be able to communicate at the stage you are when you reach our world. You must try to realise that spiritual growth is always towards maturity. There is no equality with physical age.

Now I come back to the question about at what stage in our world is awareness attained. This is difficult because awareness is a growing condition, not fixed or finite. Awareness has infinite possibilities. You cannot reach the end of it. As you increase it, you realise there is more to be attained.

It is an eternal process at work. Awareness is a gradual realisation. It is not a sudden transformation from ignorance to knowledge. It is graduated, and slowly comes as the soul is ready to reach higher stages.

"We obviously don't live as long as we could physically under better conditions. Under perfect conditions probably we could live to a hundred and fifty."

Do not confuse physical age with spiritual maturity. It is not the number of years that matters, but the growth, development and unfoldment of the soul that is temporarily manifested through the body.

It is not the plan of the Great Spirit to increase the number of physical years that your body should exist in your world.

What should happen is that when the spirit is ready the body will die, just as the apple drops from the tree when it is ripe. So forget the physical years. They do not matter.

The whole object and essence of earthly life is to enable the spirit to have the kind of exercise, education and experience that fit it to begin its life in our world.

If the spirit does not have the experience to equip it for our world, then it is like a child who has gone to school, has not learnt the lessons, and is not ready for the adult life that follows.

★ ★ ★

To a widow whose husband had laboured long in the spiritual field the guide gave this encouragement:

I am very glad to welcome you and to reassure you of fundamental truths which have provided a help in your hour of difficulty and trial.

It is not easy for people in your world, even when they have knowledge that life is continuous after physical death, to adjust themselves when those who are closest to them are removed to another dimension of the universe.

It would be foolish to minimise the fact that inevitably there is sorrow when this physical separation takes place. But it is only a physical separation and not a spiritual one.

Death is inevitable for everyone in your world. There

comes a time when you have to say farewell to earth, for it has no more to offer you and the soul is ready for the adventures that are an essential part of its evolution towards perfection.

How you comport yourself when the trial comes is a question you have to decide. I know it is not easy.

Death cannot separate those whom love has joined. Love, like life, is undying. And love, like life, is a mighty force that can work its will as conditions make it possible. Of course there are times in the silence when tears are shed. But hold your head high, and know that the power of the spirit will never desert you. Help will always be forthcoming.

Do not worry about anything. Worry blocks the channels by which help can come.

You may not always realise it, but you are very fortunate because when you plumbed the depths of sorrow you were ready to receive knowledge. It was not easy to come out of the depths, but the way was shown. Now you are completely certain that the one you love is as close to you as it is possible for any human being to be.

I always wish that people in your world, especially those who have this knowledge, could become aware of what is around and about them. If only they could see the ones they love who are close to them, shielding them, guarding them, guiding them, ensuring that no real harm will ever befall them.

If you could realise the extent of this radiance you would never have any doubts or fears as to what the morrow will bring. So you should, as I always tell my friends, greet each new day as the herald of wonderful spiritual adventures.

Your life has been transformed by the evidence you have received. I know, because I have seen it, that you labour to help others as you were helped. Do not bother about what others say. That does not matter. What matters is the way you conduct your life; do the best you can and serve wherever you can.

Your man is freed from the thraldom of the flesh. He will never again suffer the aches and disabilities that proved such a nuisance to him in the last days of his earthly existence.

He will make you aware of his continued presence in what he still regards as home. So keep a stout heart, hold your head high and continue to be an exemplar of how to behave when death removes the one who is closest to you.

The separation is physical, not spiritual. There is nothing in your world or mine that can part those whom love has united. Love, like life, is stronger than death. Love, like life, is of the spirit, and the spirit cannot be destroyed.

6: What Will Happen When You Die?

One day your spirit, the God-given life-spark, will leave the physical body it adopted to allow it to function on this planet.

What will your new life beyond the earth-plane be like?

Asked how a spirit-world resident would occupy his time, Silver Birch replied:

★   ★   ★

We have no day or night. We are not dependent on the rotation of the earth's axis. We do not revolve around the sun. We have eternal light. So we do not have hours as you do on earth.

Do we work? Of course, because we love to work. We love to serve.

You will come to our world and work there, but it will be work that you enjoy. You will not have to do it to earn money, to pay the rent, to buy clothes, to buy food.

There are always people coming to our world with gifts and talents and faculties that were never manifested before. They can give them full expression and enrich the lives of the many in our world.

Each does whatever he wants to do. There is an infinite number of pursuits for the spirit. If he likes music, he can study all the compositions of your world and those of ours. We have concerts. If he is interested in literature, we have access to all the literature of your world and in ours. Art, painting – we have access to all the masterpieces produced in your world and in ours.

If he is interested in children, he can look after those who come into our world and precede their parents. If he is interested in sick souls, he can help to tend them and nurse them towards spiritual health. There is an infinite number of tasks we have for individuals to perform. Then there are others like myself who spend their time working in your world.

Once you leave your world you have a richness awaiting you that it is almost impossible to describe. We are not limited in music to your scales. We are not limited in art to your colours. It is very difficult to convey all this.

★   ★   ★

"When we pass to the spirit world do we take any form or shape as we have in the material world?"

You won't be a ghost, spectre or phantom. You won't be headless. You won't have your head under your arm. You won't have clanking chains. You will be a real individual with a body, and features which enable you to be recognised by others. You will have all the senses that will enable you to recognise others. You will have the entire spiritual apparatus which is necessary for you to function in our world.

You will have form, you will have shape, you will have individuality. What you will not have are any of the physical organs, but you will have correspondingly all the spiritual equipment necessary for you to function in our world.

What you must appreciate is that to you matter is solid and tangible, and spirit is shadowy and insubstantial. In our world spirit is the reality, is tangible, and matter is the shadowy and the insubstantial.

You do not have any of the apparatus to make you speak because you do not have to speak. All our communication is done by thought. We send our thoughts to one another and we are able to communicate as a result. Thought is a reality in our world. Everything that exists is created out of thought. And thus you can have whatever you deem necessary for as long as you want it.

We have oceans, seas, mountains, lakes, and flowers, plants, trees, animals and birds. We have beauty of the kind that you cannot appreciate until you come to our world.

It would be the exception to find in our world anyone evolved to some maturity who would hanker after the world of matter.

Another advantage is that we do not have the problems that confront you. We do not have to buy provisions, or clothes. We do not have to pay for houses. All these exist in our world.

"Do greed and desire for power exist in the spirit world since there are no material possessions?"

Greed and power still exist in what may be called the lower astral spheres. What you must recognise is that spiritually an individual is exactly the same one day after death as he was before it. Our world, unlike yours, is one where thought is the reality. What you think is real and substantial.

When we look at you, what is physical to us is shadowy; what you think, to us is real. This is hard to convey, but it is just the same as when you sleep and dream. Whatever appears in your dream is real whilst you are dreaming it. If you never woke, then everything happening in your dream would be your reality.

The ship on which you travel, the aeroplane which transports you from one place to another, the countries you visit, all this is your reality.

In our world thought is the building material that creates everything that exists. So whatever you think is there. People who come here with greed and desire for power still have them until they learn that it is useless. When they are ready to be released from this earth-bound condition, they can be helped.

The trouble is that lust for power and greed chain them to earth. Though materially dead, they are spiritually dead as well. They are nearer to your world than they are to us. Unfortunately they can harm those like themselves in your world who are concerned only with greed and power.

"Does this mean that more and more of such spirit entities become nearer to this world, and is also a reason why our earth is in such a difficult period?"

Yes, because you must understand that our world is composed of the people who come to it from your world. We have no other inhabitants in our spheres than those who come to us from your earth. As long as you allow people to come to us unready, unprepared, unevolved and unfit, so you are creating trouble in your world and in ours.

That is why we are at work to bring enlightenment to your world, so that it will help to end the violence, greed, materialism, selfishness and avarice, all those dreadful cancers which are responsible for war, disharmony and disruption everywhere.

"You said the spirit world is populated by people coming from this globe. Is your spirit world located right round our globe, or does it extend further? And do various spirit worlds exist?"

The Great Spirit is infinite. Life is infinite. Your little world is a speck in the cosmos.

"So are there various earths and spirit worlds?"

There are spheres and spheres of existence. You are not alone in the universe.

"If you were asked to describe where the Other Side is, how would you reply? It is so difficult to give a tangible answer."

It is the invisible and inaudible side of the world in which you live. You are as much now in the world of spirit as ever you will be. You will not go there when you pass from your world; you are in the spirit world now. You cannot register it unless you have developed the gifts of the spirit so that you can tune in to all its vibrations and frequencies, or whatever word you care to use. It is not another world. It is an integral part of the universe of which earth is but one aspect.

"Would it be true to say it is our job while we are on earth so to develop the finer side that we become aware of the invisible world?"

Yes. You really begin to enjoy life when you are aware not only of the material aspect but the spiritual aspect as well. If you are unaware of the spiritual reality then, alas, spiritually you are deaf, dumb and blind.

"You say that when you come to our world it is darker. So you must come from somewhere."

It is a change in the mode of manifestation. It is a slowing down of our usual vibratory rates. We have to discard some of the elements of our being which belong to higher octaves of vibration, so that we can register in your lower octaves.

★ ★ ★

"For what reason is there a spirit world and a physical world? Why is there not just the spirit world?"

The answer is for me to say to you, "Why do you send children to school?"

This is done so that in their schooldays they learn the lessons that will equip them for the life they must lead when they leave, and are confronted with very different conditions. That is the reason why you come into the physical world. It provides the opportunities and challenges for you to equip yourself for the life you must lead when you leave your world. It is a process of learning so that you are ready for the next stage.

The physical world, the spirit world, the universe, the seemingly endless cosmos, all these are the creation of a supreme power which you call God and I call the Great Spirit. It is the mightiest power that exists. It is infinite; it has neither beginning nor end. Its wisdom is infinite, its love is infinite, its storehouse is infinite.

The natural laws for which the Great Spirit is responsible are supreme in their operation. There is no circumstance that has ever happened, or will ever happen, for which provision has not been made.

The laws of your world are subject to constant change

and revision because unforeseen conditions arise.

The natural laws are perfect. There is nothing outside their operation. They encompass everybody and everything no matter how majestic or minute, complex or simple. They are all regulated by natural, unchanging, unbreakable law.

That is why I pay tribute to the Supreme Power because there is nothing and none that can compare with its sublimity and profundity. The intelligence responsible is of a magnificence that is impossible to put in earthly language.

I who have lived much longer than any of you constantly marvel at the way in which the natural laws operate in every sphere of being.

And so I say to you that whatever exists does so because it has a purpose to serve. If you live in harmony with these natural laws you will derive the supreme benefits that come in health, well-being, spiritual radiance and mental excellence because you will be expressing some of that latent divinity within you. It is important to recognise that you are attempting to understand with a finite mind that which pertains to infinity.

"Do you communicate with the Great Spirit?"

Not as you understand 'communicate.' Your communication has to be done verbally, by writing or by mechanical means. You have to use language to make yourselves understood. Language is finite and cannot express the totality of that which is infinite. Even the greatest masters of literature cannot put in words the infinity of the universe and all that it contains.

In the higher reaches of our world, communication is

direct from mind to mind. Do we communicate with the Great Spirit? No, not in the sense in which communication means the use of language. We commune. We try to harmonise ourselves with the infinite power, and receive as much as we can from all it has to offer.

"Do you think you are closer to the power than we are?"

You are all close to the Great Spirit because the Great Spirit is within you. You live only because a part of the Great Spirit has given you life.

When you talk of closeness, do you mean that you can establish a greater attunement and harmony with the Great Spirit? The answer is yes, because spirit is infinite and perfect. But it cannot express its perfection at any stage of your being either in your world or in ours.

* * *

"You say perfection is never attained; there is a constant striving towards it. Is this because perfection is an aspect of duality? Are there spheres or states of consciousness beyond the laws of duality? If so these must surely be beyond their comprehension."

In the nature of the case perfection cannot be attained because the question would be what happens after you attain it, when you reach the stage where you have nothing more to achieve. Perfection is an infinite process. It is the constant elimination of dross to allow the pure gold of the spirit to emerge. You cannot put a period to infinity; you cannot put a full stop to eternity.

It is like knowledge. The more you learn the more you learn there is to be learned. You cannot arrive at the summit of all knowledge. There is an infinite number of planes, levels or spheres of consciousness. This is an attribute of the spirit which, being infinite, means there will always be a constant development.

You use the word "duality." What do you mean by it?

"The law of opposites."

What I call polarity. There are natural laws conceived by infinite intelligence and wisdom that have made arrangements for every possible circumstance. The natural laws never have to be changed or repealed. Their very nature is evidence of infinite intelligence at work. It is wonderful to reflect that there will always be more to achieve. There is no nirvana, no stage of bliss when you have come to the end of your spiritual progress.

"Are there laws beyond the laws of cause and effect which we possibly cannot comprehend at this time?"

There are laws, but they are part of the same unity that rules cause and effect.

"When you are away from this circle, at what level of consciousness do you function? How great is your awareness?"

We are in the realm of the incomprehensible. In the spiritual realm you are in states which are beyond earthly language and require an inner realisation of what is being experienced. When I leave your world and withdraw into the level or sphere which is my natural habitat, I am expressing a developed consciousness that cannot be manifested when I communicate on earth. It is a degree of spiritual realisation that cannot be measured in language that you would understand.

A circle visitor remarked:

"Many enigmas perplex me when it comes to verifying the truth of life's continuity. I try to imagine how this could manifest. Is it a form of energy, a thought, or any thing that

has a body similar to the one that we now have?"

When I look around your world I sometimes wonder whether there is life before death! There are millions who do not seem to be living at all or, if they are, express themselves in the most minute form that is possible.

It is very difficult to convey what life in our world is like because we live in dimensions that are beyond what you can comprehend in your limited state. Language is inadequate to convey what is beyond the three dimensions of being with which you are familiar.

I cannot possibly express the richness of living that exists in our world because there are not sufficient comparisons that can be made. It is a world where the aspirations, dreams and hopes of those who seek to develop the fullness of being are realised. Gifts that were stultified on earth are expressed.

We do not have economic problems, we do not have social problems, we do not have colour or racial problems. We are concerned not with bodies but with souls. And souls do not have colours of white, red, yellow or black.

We have spheres or conditions of being that are graded according to the evolution of those who dwell in them. You reach that sphere for which you are spiritually ready, not higher, because that is impossible; not lower, because you would not desire it unless you wish to perform some missionary service.

As awareness increases, the individual realises that he or she possesses infinite possibilities, that the road to perfection is an endless one. The regrets experienced come when they contemplate the mistakes they made, the services they should have rendered, the hurts for which they were responsible, and do their best to make amends.

There is an inevitable law of compensation and retribution. It works in every case. The natural law is perfect; none can evade it. Pretence is stripped away; all is known. There is nothing for the sincere aspirant to fear.

Problems you will always have. They are there because in solving them you grow. If there were no problems you would cease to be alive in any sense of the word. The soul comes into its own not in the sunshine, but in the storm.

If I were to say to you we will banish your difficulties I would not be talking the truth. What I can teach you is how to face and conquer them. There is no difficulty or obstacle so large that you have no power, combined with ours, to overcome it. Even when I cannot communicate according to the fashion of your world I still am with you because the problems of space and time that encumber you do not apply to us. We can reach you wherever you are. We will continue to help you to the utmost limits of our strength.

"To have compensation and retribution would imply that, for example, you get paid for what you have achieved. Where is the God who preordains things?"

How could divine justice work without compensation and retribution? Is the sinner to have equality of spiritual status with the saint? Of course not. Whatever good you do, you are the better for it. Whatever selfishness you have shown, you are the worse for it.

It is you who make or mar your spiritual destiny. It is

you who are personally responsible. If on your deathbed you could repent, and by so doing automatically get rid of all the imperfections that result from sins committed, that would be a mockery and a travesty.

"Provided I was responsible for choosing the implements. I have no way of choosing them."

How do you know?

"Only by my personal awareness."

That is only a tiny fraction of the awareness you have. You made your choice before you incarnated into this world of yours, when you had a fuller awareness than you have now. So you must make the best of it.

"With the little I have?"

No, you must make the best of the lot you have. You are very fortunate. The way was shown to you when you needed it most.

You would not be where you are now were it not that the finger of the spirit pointed the way for you at the greatest crisis of your earthly life.

You have been richly blessed with that knowledge which cannot be bought in any market in your world. You have a knowledge of spiritual reality. It says in the book called the Bible, "Add to your faith knowledge." I say, "Add to your knowledge faith."

* * *

A frequent criticism of mediumship is that descriptions of the next world differ.

Silver Birch told circle visitors:

You have to realise that we live in an infinite world and thus there must be an infinite variety of experiences for its dwellers. Life in our world is graded spiritually and thus there are differences of experience for all who are here.

Anyone communicating with you can transmit only what he or she has experienced at that time. With progress, that soul will move to another plane of being which can cause him or her to revise an opinion previously held.

So it depends on the evolution of the communicator as to what pictures are being transmitted to your world. You must remember that the closer the communicator is to your world, the more limited is the ability to express what is higher in the scale of spiritual values which he or she has yet to attain.

Everything existing in that realm in which an individual dwells is available for examination. The conditions pertaining in higher spiritual realms are something he cannot appreciate and so of necessity he is restricted to what is apparent to him. He can go lower, but not higher.

My advice is always the same. Treat every communication from our world with reason. If your common sense says, "No, I cannot accept this," then reject it. We are not infallible. We have not attained perfection, because that requires eternity. The process, as I have already said, is infinite.

I never say to my friends here or to visitors: "This is what you must do. This is what you must believe." We are not dictators; we are co-operators. We have to win you with truth, wisdom, logic, reason and love, knowing that if we can gain your love then we have achieved our task.

Ours is a religion of truth. We have only truth to offer, as we understand it, as it has been revealed to us and to you. We may be clumsy in our attempts to express it because we, like you, are human and subject to error and imperfection.

But we will continue to instil into you what we regard as eternal, unbreakable, immutable, spiritual principles on which the whole of life is founded. We say to you that if you live according to the spiritual laws then no real harm can ever befall you.

You will not escape the difficulties and trials and troubles of earthly life, because they are essential to your evolution. You must experience the darkness in order to enjoy the light. You must experience rain in order to appreciate the sun. You must have the polarities that life has to offer, because if it were only one monotone there would be no appreciation and no development either physically, mentally or spiritually.

The Great Spirit, with infinite wisdom, has bestowed on you the gift of reason. Use it at all times. Do not be afraid to dismiss anything which comes to you from our world that makes your reason revolt.

"Is my idea correct of this life being a classroom to which we will return?"

If you have not learned the lessons you will have to return to it to do so.

You can look back and see how the signposts of the spirit have pointed the way when you thought no direction was forthcoming.

That is how the power of the spirit works. You are never left alone. Always there are not only those you love to guide you, but kindred souls not related by ties of blood who have a spiritual affinity with you. They see in you instruments capable of rendering service to the

Great Spirit by serving the Great Spirit's children in your world.

* * *

"If I wanted to learn to play the piano in your world would I have to take lessons?"

Of course you would. You do not get anything for nothing. We have advanced tutors who can help according to the talents that you possess. Often our life gives a tremendous opportunity to newly-arrived dwellers who had gifts, talents and faculties which they could not possibly develop in your world through economical or social circumstances. Now they are free to allow these talents to reach their fullest heights.

"You have no need of sleep. Do you rest and have periods of relaxation?"

Yes, whenever we feel the need for relaxation.

"How is your spirit sustained and kept going – through access to the Great Spirit?"

We do not have physical bodies that require to be sustained by food.

"Is there some spiritual equivalent?"

Yes, we have the whole of the power of the spirit on which to draw. The spirit is infinite.

"Of course we will have to wait until we get to your side to understand this."

That is true. Then you will have the same difficulty in describing it to others.

"We know without doubt that we go to your world. We have learned from you that knowledge has tremendous implications. While we are here we have to live those implications. We know that all of us have spiritual gifts of some kind and

our function here is to try to develop them. Would it be true to say that this is all we can concern ourselves with whilst we are here?"

It is impossible to convey a non-physical spiritual world in physical terms because your thinking, all your mental concepts, are restricted by language and by an awareness only of the world in which you live.

Your five senses, wonderful as they are, restrict what you can possibly receive, and assimilate when you have received it. The mystic is aware of the greater reality that is behind the surface of life. But to try to explain that awareness is futile because language is artificial and inspiration is beyond earthly language.

"Can you tell us what communication is like between the spirit spheres?"

As I tried to say before, the trouble is that we have to use language to express reality that is beyond language. The use of the word "sphere" is in itself a difficulty. You think of a sphere as a globe, but it is a condition, a state, a stage.

All life in our world is graduated. Each stage merges into one that is higher, and this is a continuous process. There are no rigid lines of demarcation between one sphere and another. There are no geographical areas.

It is not possible for those who dwell in one sphere to communicate with those who are in spheres that are spiritually higher. But it is possible for those in the spiritually superior spheres to communicate with those in the lower ones. The method of communication is mind to mind. We do not speak, because we do not have the physical apparatus for producing voices. It is a communication of thought to thought.

"Is there no privacy of thoughts in the spirit world?"

No, you cannot conceal anything in our world, for all is known. In that, there is nothing to be ashamed. In your world you can cheat, lie and deceive. You can change your name legally if you like, but you cannot change your individuality.

A visitor remarked that spirit entities communicating at his home circle often announced they had borne famous names.

In our world names do not matter. An earthly fame has no value. Souls judge themselves not by their titles, but by what they did, which results in the character that they have. The only passport in our world is the stage of the development of your soul, which is naked for all to see.

You cannot cheat; you cannot lie; you cannot pretend. When you come here, the mask of earth is stripped away and you are known for what you are. All can perceive the spiritual stage you have reached.

What is fame? Fame is merely a bauble. It has no value. Why do some people achieve fame in your world? Because they made money, or are materially successful. Jesus of Nazareth never sought fame. The great teachers, mystics, saints, pioneers and reformers, did they seek fame?

It is the service that matters, not the name you bear. So beware of those who come to you with so-called famous names. The test is not what you say, but what you do and what you teach.

I have said constantly that if I propound sentiments which insult your intelligence or make your reason revolt, reject them. If we cannot win you with love, and because what we say bears the mark of truth, then we have failed.

★ ★ ★

Answering a question as to why a close relative has never returned, the guide said:

There is free will. There is no compulsion to come back. It is not a very attractive world to return to when you have tasted some of the ineffable joys, beauty and radiance that are available in our world. It requires a sacrifice to return, to approach earth's atmosphere, which is gloomy, dark, dank and most unwelcoming.

"Would a telepathic contact, if it could be made, involve a spirit in suffering? Can the spirit be contacted in his own plane?"

Yes, it is always possible. We would be very happy if spirit communication were achieved in which you on earth met the people in our world returning half-way. Alas, it does not happen very often. It has to be a descent into your atmosphere, your conditions, your vibrations. The spiritual has to be made material. We would like to see the material become spiritual.

★ ★ ★

"I have heard of astral travelling, which seems to happen to me. How does this function?"

It happens very simply that the real you leaves your body and is able to travel vast distances, sometimes into our world, and sometimes into the further reaches of your world. Actually, every one of you travels astrally when you go to sleep. Then your spirit, for the time being, departs from your body, roams into our world and meets souls you love and who love you. It is a divine provision by which preparation is made for the time when you come here, so that it will not be a shock. When you do come you will remember, and be ready for the many wonderful happenings that spirit life has to offer you. It could be said that you die every night.

"Everybody dreams at night. Often we remember we have met people we know who were near to us. Do we really meet these people, or is it just imagination, or a wish that we would like to meet them?"

No, you actually meet those who have preceded you into my world. Do not disparage imagination. It has its poor side, but also its rich side. Imagination, when used in the highest, best and purest form, is a great gift. It is the creative means by which untapped faculties and gifts can gradually blossom into a fuller expression.

Not all dreams are memories of spirit experiences. There are also the ones which are merely the result of what is stored in the subconscious mind, or sometimes caused by the food you eat too late at night.

"Can we tell the difference?"

Yes, because the food you eat late at night and what is in your subconscious mind do not bring any spiritual verities with them. When you carry back impressions of loved ones you have met, this will bring a mental and spiritual warmth which enables you to differentiate very clearly indeed.

Development is required to know the difference between a purely physical impression and a spiritual impression. One is like having a heavy thud on your shoulder; the other is like being kissed by a butterfly.

★ ★ ★

"I have been told that in the spirit world a person can do many things in different places at the same time. Is it something to do with the group soul, that everything each facet of this diamond does seems to each individual facet as if he were doing it himself?"

In our world its dwellers can express varying aspects of life, but not be in several different aspects at the same time. They can only be in one place at one time.

We are not subjected to the limitations of travel that are imposed on you because of physical conditions. If, for example, we want to visit remote places in your world that physically are thousands of miles away, that presents no problem; we can be there instantly.

It has nothing to do with being a facet of a diamond or an integral part of a group soul. The facets of the diamond incarnate into your world to acquire experiences that will help the diamond.

"So in totality the diamond is a better one as a result."

Yes, because it has increasing awareness and unfoldment. It has been enriched by what the facets have done in your world. Earth is essentially a part of spiritual progress. If it were not, then it would not exist.

"Do I presume there is no time in the spirit world as we know it?"

No, because your relationship to time is governed by the rotation of the earth round the sun which gives you day and night and seasons. We are not subject to earth's rotations, therefore we do not have day and night and different seasons. Time, as you know it, does not exist for us. We live in what can best be described as an eternal present.

"And an eternal past?"

As far as we are concerned the past and future are part of the eternal present.

It is not so difficult if you realise what happens in sleep, when your mind is freed temporarily from physical limitations. In your dreams you defeat these limitations altogether, and travel vast distances. You annihilate time, as you understand it in your world. And all of this happens within seconds or minutes.

"We seem bound by time in this life, yet quite obviously the spirit world is timeless."

Time itself has no past or future. Time is in the eternal present. It is only your relationship to time which makes your past and your future.

You are living in a world of three dimensions. We are not dependent on the earth's axis, on a spinning globe which makes your day and night. We live in eternal light. How can I convey this to you? We do not have to go to sleep because we have no physical bodies like you. We do not have bodies that require sleep. If we require rest, we just pause until we feel invigorated.

Ours is a richer, more beautiful world that you can possibly visualise. How can I describe a world in which there are octaves of sound that do not come within your range of hearing, or sights that are not limited by your spectrum of vision? It is too difficult, I know, but it exists.

You have to be bound by physical laws because you are incarnated into matter. You are spirits; you have a soul, and that is greater than anything physical. Spirit is master and matter is servant. Spirit is superior and matter is not the enduring reality.

When your spirit vacates it, your physical body will

crumble into dust. It will change its form; it will not be a physical body again. You, the spirit, will emerge radiant, not dependent on a heart and liver and lungs. Your spirit will provide the energy, the sustenance for all that you require.

7: *Music of the Spheres*

Music plays a subtle part in the Divine Plan.

Silver Birch gave a leading musician a foretaste of the delights awaiting him in the Beyond.

★ ★ ★

What you can never appreciate is the service you render with the music you provide. Music, especially of the inspired kind which is natural for you to transmit to others, has a great healing, soothing, stimulating, uplifting quality. In its way that too can touch souls and make them realise there is a sublimity of life far greater than any of the things that the physical senses can perceive or comprehend.

Whenever you play in future remember you are an instrument of a great purpose, helping to bring harmony, sympathy, stimulation, happiness and health to many others who cannot convey their thanks to you.

You have the greatest treat due when you reach our world, because we have music of a quality and superiority you cannot now comprehend. We have octaves of sound that you have never heard in your world. We have symphonies, we have concertos, we have orchestras and we have the greatest music makers and masters in our world. You have only a few in yours.

We have access not only to the great music makers,

but they have evolved since coming to our world. There is greater music performed for those who are ready to appreciate it. Our halls of music are among the treasures of our life. You will hear octaves of sound that are incapable of being registered by any of your instruments.

And of course the music that enriches your world has its source in our world. It is not created in your world. Musicians and composers are the mediums.

"It is a great privilege to be here. I very much want to tell you that your teachings are a wonderful inspiration in my life."

Let us both thank the Great Spirit, I for the opportunity and privilege of service and you and your wife for being able to receive it.

I came to your world many years ago, a lone figure without a friend.

I was asked if I would return to your world under these difficult conditions, forfeiting whatever I had earned in higher reaches of life, because there was a great need for spiritual realities and powers to be established. I accepted the challenge.

Here you are tonight telling me that the teachings which I am privileged to transmit – they do not originate from me – have helped you. I am grateful for that knowledge. It shows that I have added some more friends at whose hearths I can feel the warmth of their love, and that means a great deal to me.

You will be given many opportunities to serve others as you have been served. Take them when you can. I am not asking you or anybody to become an evangelist, a missionary seeking to make converts whenever possible. We do not wish you, or any others associated with us, to play on the emotions of the masses, to arouse them with fervour to accept things which in the cold light of day for many of them will prove unreasonable.

What we do say is that you will be provided with opportunities to help those who come into your orbit. Then do the best you can for them. There is a great work to be done in your world.

Material possessions can only be your temporary belongings. You are merely their custodians. Those of a spiritual nature will not rust or tarnish; they will endure. There is no religion higher than service, which is the coin of the spirit. Those who serve others less fortunate than we are will find that the way will be shown. There will be brought to them people they can help in their time of crisis, just as you were guided when you needed it.

★ ★ ★

Referring to discordant and technical modern music, a visitor asked if inspiration had changed its form.

Inspiration does not change. Inspiration is constant, but it can be received only by those who are ready to do so, and they must be attuned to that wavelength on which it can operate. Inspiration is always at work. Like spirit power, it seeks to find avenues through which it can express itself.

It is a question of attunement. You must recognise that in your world there are pioneers in all forms of art, in music and in painting. Sometimes they are so much in advance that the people of their time are unable to appreciate it. But with the years that pass, understanding comes, and recognition is afforded to the pioneers.

That does not apply to the vulgarisation of music that often takes place in your world. This is in line with the violence that is part of the cancerous growth infesting your world today.

"I wondered if the generation was affecting the music."

You cannot divorce matter from spirit because each reacts and interacts so far as the other is concerned. Your body affects your spirit, and your spirit affects your body. They are not in watertight compartments.

"Jung says everything that happens on the inside must manifest itself on the outside. Is some of the modern, violent, tuneless music evidence of this? Is it not better out than in? Does it help to dissipate the violence?"

No, it is a natural reaction, unfortunately. It is an expression of the material, part of the selfishness, the complete unconcern for the welfare of others. It is greed at work. That explains the violence afflicting itself on your world. And that violence is expressed not only in physical behaviour, but in music, art, and in every other form of life.

8: The Divine Mission

Silver Birch's teachings, available in print for decades, have reached millions all over the world.

To add a second dimension, his words were recorded at one seance, bringing the serene eloquence of his distinctive voice, so different from his medium's, into thousands of homes.

After his customary invocation, Silver Birch explained his mission.

★　★　★

I am very happy to come amongst you and to bring my love and greetings from the world of spirit.

I am aware of the special purpose of our gathering tonight. So I thought it might be helpful if I would try to explain to those who will hear these words the purpose behind my mission and those of my colleagues who are animated by the same desire.

To the uninitiated I would say I am a human being like yourselves. I have lived much longer than any of you who are listening to what I say. As a result of my experiences in realms far beyond your earth I have gained some knowledge of the Great Spirit you call God, and of the natural laws which have been devised to ensure that the will of the Great Spirit will and must ultimately prevail.

What I have learnt as a result of my experiences I am willing to share with those who are ready to receive them because I think they may be of helpfulness to them.

I am not in any way a deity, I am still very human, capable of error, weakness and imperfection. I have, like every one of you, a long, long way to go on the road to perfection. It is an infinite one.

But, like others in my world, I was asked to retrace my steps so that I could offer some of the truth, the wisdom and the knowledge that we have gained, and share it with you. At the same time we would be able, with the aid of those who co-operate with us, to make available the supreme power of the spirit, which is responsible for all life despite its multitudinous forms, so that this power can stream through gifted individuals and serve its benign purpose.

In olden days, when this power flowed, it performed certain remarkable phenomena which many today regard as miracles. I want to say that in the operation of natural law they cannot be suspended or abrogated, and must fulfil themselves in an ordered sequence as effect follows cause.

Whatever has happened, however remarkable, stupefying, extraordinary or wonderful in days gone by, it was due to the operation of natural laws.

These operate not only in the physical domain but also work ceaselessly in the spiritual realms. When conditions allow, the spiritual, psychic, astral and etheric laws can be brought into operation to perform what were regarded as miracles yesterday, but today are described as psychic phenomena produced through mediumship.

A medium is one on whom there has been bestowed

the gifts of the spirit which are ably described by the apostle Paul in your Bible. These gifts are divinely bestowed. Their recipients, as they unfold them, are able to be used as channels for the divine beneficence to flow through them.

All the phenomena of mediumship are due to the operation of spirit power. Today you are witnessing exactly the same kind of manifestations that occurred in the lands which were called holy and regarded as sacred.

The Great Spirit does not change; the natural laws do not alter. They are in operation now. Thus I, who once inhabited your world, am able to speak to you through a medium by utilising the same power of the spirit.

I want to explain also that we are part of a vast spirit organisation. We are pursuing what I would like to describe as the overall master plan, which is designed to ensure that the power of the spirit will continue to express itself in your world and reach an ever increasing number of people. The object is to drive away their ignorance, error and superstition and to bring them into the radiant light of divine truth and knowledge so that they can begin to live and fulfil themselves as they should according to the purpose of their earthly incarnation.

The power of the spirit has constantly flowed into your world from time immemorial; its descent, however, was only temporary and sporadic. The wonders that were worked, the signs that were given, the same truths that were pronounced were each time made available to the people of that day.

Then there was decay, tampering with the knowledge that had been revealed, for political, theological, and sometimes state purposes. Now, however, the power of the spirit, because of the overall plan to which I have referred, is here to stay in your world.

Why? Because it is vitally necessary to do so. So many systems have failed to provide the direction which will enable the people who dwell on earth to find themselves, and to live according to ideals that will enable the divinity which gave them life to express itself. The spirit has to be made prominent in the lives of all who dwell on earth.

It is a very dark world in which you live. It is full of turbulence, violence, greed, envy. Mammon is being worshipped instead of the Great Spirit. False idols are still the ones which are the subject of adoration.

The evidence that is available to you will, if you are reasonable, convince you that life, because it is spiritual in essence, cannot end when death comes to the physical body.

Matter is only the husk; the spirit is the reality. Matter exists only because spirit animates it. When spirit, the life force, withdraws, matter crumbles into dust. But the spirit, which is the individual, does not crumble into dust. The spirit is immortal; it cannot die. Death is its second birth.

Its first came when it was born into your world and began to manifest through a physical body. The second birth comes when the spirit says farewell to the physical body and continues in unbroken sequence its eternal path on the road of infinite progress. You cannot die. Life is deathless.

So there is the evidence that you, an individual, immortal spirit, will continue after the death of your body. Everything that constitutes your individuality will persist. You will have consciousness, awareness, memory, the power to reason and to express love, for love is an aspect of the Great Spirit.

Love in its highest form is divine, and love, like life, is deathless.

Why do we come back to you? It would be easy to say farewell for ever to earth with all its heartaches, its problems, its sufferings, its trials, its difficulties. But we love you, and there are others who are bound to you by ties of love just as strong.

The marriage service performed in your churches refers to the existence of the marriage until death parts the man and his wife. If spiritually they are not united they are parted before death comes. If there is love, there is nothing that will ever separate them.

Love is a mighty force in the universe. It is love that is expressed by all advanced beings in our world whose only desire is to serve you. We seek nothing for ourselves. We require no worship, no adoration, no gratitude. If we succeed in helping, all we ask is that you express your thanks to the Great Spirit and, because of what you have received, try to serve others.

The greed of your world must be replaced by love, because love is an expression of the spirit. Love has many aspects, compassion, service, friendship, co-operation. You are all parts of one another, whatever you are, whoever you are and wherever you may be.

Colour, class, nationality, language, these constitute only physical differences. Spiritually you are all members of one another. You make up the vast human spiritual family because the common link of the spirit binds you all to one another with a tie that cannot be broken, just as it binds you all to the Great Spirit.

The spirit that unites you is stronger than any of the physical differences that separate you from one another. You have to allow that spirit to express itself to its fullest capacity. You must learn self-regeneration. You must forget self, insofar as being materialistic in desire is concerned.

This is not to say that you should overlook your physical needs. You must sustain the body, which is the temple of the spirit. Equally, however, you must tend and care for all the attributes of the spirit, which is the eternal you.

You must allow the divinity within you to attain its fullest expression, so that you practise the brotherhood and sisterhood which is a natural fact of your being. The soul is not white, yellow, black or red. The soul has no colour or racial bar.

This is what you have to learn to practise. Superiority comes only when you unfold the divinity within you, and it expresses itself in love and compassion and consideration, not only for all the other humans in your world but for the animals who share this planet with you.

You must abolish needless cruelty and exploitation everywhere. Peace will come when you put into practice the facts that appertain to your spiritual origin and destiny.

In everything I say I am governed by the desire to be helpful, to bring some understanding, some knowledge, some truth and some wisdom into your lives.

It is possible that the principles that we enunciate may

be contrary to certain theological ideas of doctrines, dogmas and creeds on which you have been nurtured from childhood days.

Our appeal is directed to your reason. If there is anything we say or do that insults your intelligence or makes your reason revolt, do not accept it. We desire to win your reason, your intelligence, so that you may co-operate with us and be instruments of the Great Spirit in ensuring that the divine will must prevail. You will help to speed the coming of peace in your world.

As you learn to fulfil yourselves you will obtain as a result a richness, radiance, steadfastness, resolution, awareness and inner peace. You will be in harmony with the laws that the Great Spirit devised, and even with the Great Spirit, a portion of whose divinity is within each one of you.

★ ★ ★

Silver Birch was asked if there were any final words he would like to say to those who would hear the cassette made of this sitting.

I would like to give my love to all my friends, many of whom I have not met. I would like them to know that I appreciate the love and affection that come to me from them and make it possible for me to work in your world. It is not an easy task; it is a wonderful challenge which I have accepted.

Your world is cold, it is drear, it is dismal, it is dark. But here and there throughout your earth we find places where there are the human hearths of love, affection and friendship where we can warm ourselves and enjoy the radiance that is offered by these lighthouses of the spirit in your world.

For others who are newcomers, I say: "Pray for guidance, pray for knowledge, pray for truth, and it will come to you." It has been said truly, "Ask and you shall receive, knock and it shall be opened unto you."

May the blessing of the Great Spirit be with you always.

9: Diamond of the Soul

Knowing her courage in facing the problems caused by her husband's illness, Silver Birch invited a former visitor to return to the circle.

One of her difficulties concerned the enigma of reincarnation.

★ ★ ★

I don't have to tell you this is your testing time in which you are being tried to the utmost. But you will come through no matter what difficulties surround you. The power that is behind you is a mighty one. It will not fail you.

In all earthly life there are times when you meet with the great challenges in which you come face to face with the stark realities of life in your world.

It is then that you have to make sure that your beliefs are founded on unshakeable knowledge. This can provide the means of ensuring that you will play your part and in no way allow any happening, however near and close, to deflect you from what you know is the undeniable reality of life, the fact that it is founded on spiritual principles which cannot fail.

And you are fortunate in that the preparation has been made because you were led to obtain the knowledge which is the bulwark for you in this time of crisis.

So you must continue to hold your head high. Show

by your demeanour and bearing that you will not in any way be diverted from the truth that has brought you spiritual freedom.

"I have problems with my children though they are both coping. The youngest is very interested in Spiritualism and psychic matters.

"My husband does not believe and is very upset that I do not discourage my son's interest. He is distressed because it is so against anything he believes. I do not know whose needs are greater."

I think the need of youth is greater than the beliefs of age.

One is at the stage where the earthly life has almost reached its course. The other is at the beginning, when the whole course has still to be run. Use your tact and diplomacy, as you have done, but do not in any way swerve from the principles that you know to be true.

You realise that stifling natural psychic faculties is not advisable. If they are allowed to stultify, then there is disharmony in the make-up of the child. It is always preferable to achieve wholeness rather than to allow what should be natural not to find its expression. But you can do it in your own way and help your man as you have helped him considerably.

"This child seems to believe in the principles of reincarnation. But he is worried now because he knows his father is dying. He cannot understand how when he dies he can be reunited with the family if it is split."

It is not such a problem because there may be a very long interval before reincarnation occurs. They say in your world, and it is an axiom I accept, that you should never cross your bridge until you come to it.

Reincarnation is a truth which has many facets. Because of that it is not easy to explain the complexity of reincarnation to minds which are unable to accept all that is involved.

I have never hesitated in proclaiming that I maintain reincarnation is a fact. I have not said that it is so for everybody. What I have said is that the human individuality is not always a single entity but a facet of a larger diamond.

These facets incarnate into your world for experience that will enable them to return to the diamond and add to its lustre and radiance. It is part of the law of cause and effect in operation because there are karmic debts to be paid. There are also opportunities for evolved souls to return at a time when they can perform a service to groups, and even to countries, where there is a need for their qualities and gifts to be expressed.

It is a complex subject. It involves an understanding of the extent to which individuality can be appreciated because it is far more than the personality in one earthly incarnation.

There is a confusion between personality and individuality. An individual can reincarnate and have many personalities. These are the physical expressions, manifestations of the individuality, but the individuality is unchanged.

Personality, from *persona*, the mask, belongs to the physical body. It is the way that the individuality is able to express itself through the five material senses, and that is the tip of the iceberg.

Personality is the mask that you wear on earth; individuality, the real self, seldom expresses itself, through the inability to do so. At best it is only a very poor manifestation of what can be shown when it is finally divorced from the physical body.

The individuality is far greater than the personality. It is not personality that exists after physical death. Personality is only a shadow cast by the sun which is the individuality.

Individuality survives, and gradually manifests its latent potential that cannot be expressed on earth. In the case of service that is to be rendered to your world, there is a larger individuality, a diamond which has many facets. These facets incarnate so as to have expression that will add to the diamond's lustre.

Some of you will discover that you are affinities. Although you are two people you are two halves of one individuality. When that happens in your world it brings with it a richness that cannot be measured in terms of material wealth. Affinities are the facets of the diamond. These are difficult matters to explain.

You can have a soul which is the diamond of many facets. These facets, at differing eras, can incarnate into your world as personalities. But when they pass from your world and return to ours they are still facets of the one individuality.

It is not automatic that families are reunited in our world. It happens only when there is a natural spiritual affinity between their members. If this does not exist, there is no reunion possible because they are at differing levels of consciousness.

In similiar fashion a husband and wife will not be reunited in our world unless it was a marriage of souls and minds as well as bodies and brains. It is the spiritual affinity that decides in reunion. What happens is that for a time the vibrations of the blood tie persist, but not eternally.

Spirit is superior to matter. What is of the spirit will endure; what is of matter will not. You must try to explain that to your boy. It is not easy. But everything is regulated by unfailing law. Love is the key because love is the expression of the Great Spirit, God, the Lord, the Creator, whatever name you choose to use.

Hold your head high. You have been guided and helped, and you will come through. Do not allow even for one moment the thought of failure. You will be strengthened in spirit as a result and learn the very valuable lessons which will bring a great richness to you in the days that lie in front of you.

We can never promise to those we love in your world that their paths will be easy, that they will meet with no obstacles. What we do say is that every obstacle and difficulty is a challenge. If you overcome it spiritually you are better for it.

Everybody in your world has to die. It is not part of the natural law that you should live for ever physically in your world. Once the fear of death is abolished, the fear that is due to ignorance and superstition, then the people of your world will welcome death as the angel who takes them from darkness into light and provides the opportunity for expressing gifts and faculties that had no opportunity of being utilised in your world.

★ ★ ★

The guide's answers brought further questions from circle members and visitors.

"Could you please speak on the subject of the difference between spirit and soul?

"In Spiritualism's seven principles we affirm the existence of the identity of the individual continues; in order to progress it is that fragmentation of the diamond of which you have spoken?

"When we incarnate another time, could you explain how it is the soul or the part of the soul body, the oversoul, which incarnates as opposed to the individuality of the No. 1 spirit?"

That is quite a big question. The trouble is semantics, the language of trying to find words that are incapable of explaining the totality of something that is beyond language.

Words like soul and spirit are cases in point. You have to define your terms as to what you mean by them.

Let us for the sake of simple definition refer to the soul as that portion or particle, that divinity which comes from the Great Spirit, the infinite spirit.

The spirit is the vehicle of the soul; it will function far more freely once it has separated from the physical body. This is composed of matter; it imposes restrictions on what the spirit can express on earth.

So you are the souls with spirits expressing yourself through physical bodies; the personality is that aspect which can be manifested only while you are on earth.

It is only an infinitesimal part of the individuality which is the real self; this is because it has no means of fullness of expression while it is cloaked by the physical body.

"At the time of reincarnation it is that part of the spirit or soul which incarnates rather than the personality of the first spirit?"

Yes, because the personality of the first incarnation cannot be repeated. The personality finishes with physical death; it is the physical expression of the individuality.

"I understand we all had greater knowledge that we surrendered for a short time whilst we are here, and have access to it after our passing. That would answer a lot of questions."

You chose your path before you came to earth. You then had the awareness. It is dimmed by the fact that you have a physical body and a brain that is incapable of probing all the recesses that are in the subconscious part of your mind.

You must have the crisis that becomes the catalyst that begins to awaken the awareness you originally had. It will be clearer to you one day.

"Do we choose to incarnate specifically to fulfil certain things or to acquire more knowledge?"

It is done also to perform a service and develop a gift.

"Knowledge to me is a gift."

A gift is that which the Great Spirit with infinite wisdom has bestowed on you.

"I read that we incarnate at the same time in two different places. How do you see this?"

I see it that there are facets of the diamond that incarnate to bring lustre to the diamond. It cannot incarnate as a whole because no physical body could contain the wholeness of that individuality. You must make a difference between personality and individuality. Personality is merely the life as exhibited by the physical body on earth. Individuality is the totality of the soul. You cannot express the whole of that individuality in a span of 70, 80 or 90 years in your world.

Another facet of the same diamond can incarnate at the same time. But all is regulated by law and order. Don't worry about it until it happens to you.

There is for some people the desire to reincarnate. They are the ones who have some service to render, some work to perform, some karmic debt to be paid. These are the ones who are reborn into your world. It may happen more than once. Each rebirth is a facet of the large diamond which is the total self, the complete individuality.

There is no need for you to come back to your dark, dank, drear world unless you want to do so. Having found yourselves, there is no necessity to return here.

"Why in your view do some people not reincarnate, and what happens to them?"

Because they have no karmic debt to pay and no service to give. Their earthly task is finished, so there is nothing for them to return to your world to accomplish. They have finished with it, and can continue their progress in our world.

"So they do not go to any lower world. Their progress is upward, not downward."

Progress can only be upward. If it is downward it is retrogression. Progress may not be in a straight line. It could be in a spiral, but it is ascending all the time.

The natural law encompasses all, and perfect justice prevails. You can cheat the laws of your governments, but you cannot cheat the laws of the Great Spirit. All must follow what cause and effect produce for them.

Do not worry about it because it will happen just the same.

You must try to appreciate that many people believe in reincarnation as a means of adding a kind of nobility to their lives which they do not possess. It is called in your world an inferiority complex. So it is very comforting for them to believe that however lowly their present position may be, once they were of higher rank many years ago.

But it does not work that way. The natural law ensures justice always prevails. It may not work immediately in your earthly existence, but it will operate in our world because it must do so.

"Is it possible to work out a karma in your world?"

Yes, that is the most usual way.

"Why do people choose to come back to do so?"

They have debts to pay that can only be settled in your world. That is a choice, a voluntary desire to help in times of crisis in your world. Souls have incarnated to make their contribution. All is planned.

"I think I will take a chance and work out mine on the Other Side!"

You have the choice, but you must remember that free will is only relatively free. There are things that you cannot do, and there are things that you would never choose to do because the evolution you have reached determines what steps you take.

★   ★   ★

A Swiss visitor asked: "How many years or centuries have we to wait in the spirit world until we return to this earth again? Is it correct that it is 1,060 years, and that if you die as a man you return as a woman?"

Who counted them?

"I heard it at a University lecture."

It is true that people come back to your world. They reincarnate, but they do so not according to some fixed period of time but according to a plan that exists for them to do so.

Some have karmic duties to fulfil; others volunteer to return because they have a service to render to your world. If they come back as a man or woman, it is unimportant. We have no sex discrimination acts in our world!

Spiritual attainment is the only standard. It does not matter whether you are a man or a woman; it is what you do that counts.

Besides, men and women have their parts to play in complementing one another so that the two halves make the perfect whole. That is why there are affinities who find themselves, never to be parted again.

"Sometimes we return and at other times we do not."

If there is work to be done you come back to do it. If there is an unfulfilled task you come back to do it. It is all a matter of law and order. What you express on earth is only an infinitesimal fraction of your larger individuality.

"There is a boom in getting hypnotised in order to remember former incarnations. Could we learn from such experiences?"

Sometimes. And sometimes it is a form of vanity that the subconscious mind will picture the greatness that you must have achieved before, because you are not great now.

But if it is a karmic condition, it can be that you bring into this existence a difficulty or a tragedy that made a pronounced effect on your past incarnation, and by becoming aware of it you can clear the condition. That is when it is good. But a lot of it is fanciful imagination. Sometimes it is spirit controlled by the hypnotic trance.

"The medical profession seems to be keeping people alive for months when it seems they should pass over to the next life. What happens in these cases?"

No medical man can keep a person alive when it is

time for that individual to die.

"But there are cases, a girl in America, for example."

How do you know that the medical man prolonged her life? As I understand it, your doctors are uncertain when death comes. There are controversies as to the exact moment of death.

Death is final when the silver cord is severed and the spirit body leaves the physical one. That is the only time when death occurs. When that severance has taken place, no medical man can make that physical body live again.

"Does hypnotic regression provide evidence of past lives? Is spirit possession or temporary spirit control the real reason behind the phenomenon?"

It can be sometimes in what is called regression that a contact can be made with a previous physical existence, but it is not always the case that this occurs. The mind's potential is so vast that none in your world has fathomed all its recesses. It is creative, it has subconscious desires, it can lend itself to temporary spirit possession.

All these factors have to be taken into account. There can be what you call astral projection and the impingement of a series of events which are recorded in the hypnotic trance. This does not mean that the subject is necessarily expressing a past incarnation.

"In hypnotic regression an American psychologist has appeared to uncover that when people are about to incarnate into the earthly world they seem to be guided and helped either by a group they have known before, or one composed of wiser beings. Could you throw any light on this?"

Those who have service to render in your world choose to incarnate to perform it. It may take a long time for realisation to dawn. In such cases there are guardians and guides who offer their help. But I do not think that what is known as hypnotic regression will help in this respect. Surely their object is to try and uncover what are believed to be previous incarnations.

"In this particular case the psychologist questioned people on their prebirth experiences, that they would not have been in pain or had fear."

You must be very careful with all hypnotic regressions, however sincere may be the motives of the people. The essence of hypnotism is suggestibility, and therefore you must treat with a certain amount of reserve the published accounts. They do not always convey the suggestions made by the hypnotist to the hypnotised person.

10: Guiding Lights

Questioned about spirit guides, whose voluntary mission is to aid their beloved earthly charge along the path to enlightenment, Silver Birch returned to the simile of the diamond.

★ ★ ★

"Can you tell me if spirit guides in general are an extension of one's own personality on a higher scale, or whether they are separate entities?"

It is a rather complex subject. I would prefer to use the word "individuality" rather than "personality." I draw distinctions between the personality, which is physical, and the individuality which is the soul or spiritual make-up, the reality behind the mask, so to speak.

Persons are persons so far as your world is concerned, but you cannot separate spiritual individuality in the same way. There are, for example, affinities, two kindred halves of the one soul, and sometimes they incarnate at the same time.

There are also what I call facets of the one diamond. This is the over-soul, the greater individuality, and the facets are aspects of it which incarnate into your world for experiences that will add lustre to the diamond when they return to it.

Also there are people who, although separate persons, are aspects of the one individuality. For instance, my medium, his wife and myself are parts of one individual. So you can have facets of the one guide. You can call these extensions if you like, but it comes to the same thing. Only an infinitesimal part of the whole individuality can be manifested in physical form on earth.

"I receive guidance, I am aware of it and the level from which it is coming. I have not been able to know whether this is coming from a general source or a particular guide. Is there any way by which prayer or meditation can lead one to this knowledge?"

Shall I repeat words that are very familiar? When the pupil is ready the master appears. Is that not the answer? Do not bother about it. All guidance streams from the Great Spirit. Ambassadors from the hierarchy and other enlightened beings, who are kindred souls as far as you are concerned, attach themselves to you sometimes before you are born into your world.

Sometimes they make themselves known to you before you incarnate into your world; sometimes you agree with them that you will volunteer to perform certain tasks. It does not matter what names you call them. They are there. They do not leave you. Their task is as it says in your Bible, "He shall give his angels charge concerning thee."

These are the angels of light who surround their charges, whose self-imposed task is to guard, to guide, to sustain them and always to point the way to the spiritual path that ultimately leads to mastery. It is not an easy path; it is strewn with rocks and boulders. It becomes increasingly difficult as familiar landmarks have to be left behind. But as correspondingly low as you sink, so you can rise, and the heights to which you can aspire are infinite. Perfection is not a process that you will attain. It is one which you will always be in the process of attaining.

If you wish to gain the prizes of the spirit you must prepare to make sacrifices, but once attained they can never be lost.

We are aware of all your difficulties, your problems and your desires. We know that you live in a material world. We have access to the sources of supply to ensure that those who serve will never go hungry or thirsty. All that is necessary will be provided.

What we say to you and to everyone we encounter is to do the best you can; no more is expected of you. When you fall down you can pick yourself up.

"We owe a great debt to the Red Indian guides. One by one the mediums pass away and there do not seem to be any to take their places. We want more Indian guides to help us."

Sound the war cry. The means will be found when the time is right. Of course mediums will have to die and come to our world. Physical immortality is not the plan of the Great Spirit. Earth is only a transient sphere for you. It is not your permanent home.

The visitor, a healer, explained that she was worried as to what would happen when the time came for Silver Birch's medium to pass on.

Stop worrying: worry is a bad counsellor. Have no fear. The plan will fulfil itself. I look back at the beginning of my mission with just one instrument. Then I was unable to speak your language with any degree of efficiency. I realise how fortunate we are to have reached so many people.

Others will follow. They will have the means at their

disposal of reaching far more people than we have done, because of technological devices that are to come.

You cannot measure what you are achieving. These are the imponderables. You heal physical bodies but, more important, you touch souls. You allow the patient's tiny seed of divinity to be stirred into activity and begin to flower. It is a start that ultimately will enable the individual to achieve fulfilment. Rejoice at the opportunities for service you enjoy. You were born to heal.

"Just occasionally it gets a little discouraging."

I know. I have not worked in your world for all this time without being aware of human frailties. You have the divine potential, the divine armoury on which you can call. If that is not sufficient, call on us. We will not fail you.

When you feel tired, frustrated or pessimistic, withdraw from the noisy, strident clangour of your world into the silence of your soul. Gradually attune yourself to all the rich radiance that is around you. Drink in all the beauty. Experience the calm, tranquillity, repose and steadfastness that this attunement has to offer. Then, refreshed, take up the cudgels and start again.

You must continue; you cannot draw back. Give service whenever you can. Deny none who come to seek your aid. Do not look for them. They will come to you. There is no need to go out like a town crier and say, "Who wants to be healed?" They will beat a path to your door.

Those on whom the Great Spirit with infinite wisdom has conferred the gifts of the spirit should go where they are led, to reach wherever they can, and drop seeds in the hope that they will fall in fertile ground and souls will become enriched as a result. You cannot measure or estimate the work that instruments of the spirit are doing.

"I have been told I have two guides. One is Egyptian and the other a North American Indian. Is it proper to ask for your confirmation?"

I never understand why you are troubled by such matters. Do you think they are competent guardians?

"I have no doubt."

Then it does not matter where they lived, does it? It is the power that matters, the power that has shown it is divine in origin. Have implicit faith in those who love and guide you. They will not lead you astray. They will always show the way.

11: The Pilgrim's Way

Silver Birch's guests are always those who realise they have embarked upon the journey of spiritual progress.

This is how the guide encouraged a new visitor.

★ ★ ★

I always tell my friends who come here that the pilgrims on this path all follow a similar pattern.

They have to experience difficulties, problems, crises, setbacks, disappointments, and frustrations. They even plumb the depths of despair when all seems hopeless and there is not a glimmer of light in what seems to be abysmal darkness.

Then at that stage, because the soul has been touched, the individual is ready to receive. There begins the spiritual ascent out of the depths, a slow, steady movement, not necessarily always consistent and occasionally falling back, but the climb continues with the light ever increasing until finally the darkness is dispelled.

Now you are the possessor of a wondrous knowledge based not on faith but on evidence. The way was shown, guidance was received, and understanding has changed the whole direction of your earthly life.

"It has been a great privilege for me to be here. I have been a devotee of yours for twenty years. I have been led to where I am today only through knowledge of your teachings. In my hours of need I have turned to you.

"Now I want to accumulate some of this knowledge. I have tapes and many books. I want to get together a group so that I can pass on teachings to the young to bring them on the right path."

There is a plan for the whole of humanity. It was devised by evolved spiritual beings in my world. The plan is to liberate spiritually, mentally and physically all those in your world who can be reached as they are ready to be helped. It is a plan for nations and for individuals. It will gradually outwork itself, and we are not in a hurry.

When you are engaged in this sublime task which encompasses us all, you cannot be in a hurry. Too much is at stake. What we offer is evidence, and thus the knowledge of how individuals can achieve self-regeneration. We cannot save you; you have to save yourself. The means are at your disposal.

Because of the fact of your nature you have within yourself not only a portion of the Great Spirit which is infinite, but all the armoury and power of the spirit, which you can express as you evolve. What concerns us is to reach individuals one at a time as they are ready to receive. I stress this fact because it is true.

You have a saying in your world, 'You can take a horse to water, but you cannot make it drink.'

The Nazarene used even stronger language when he referred to the problem of trying to cast pearls before swine.

Individuals must be ready to receive. You were not ready to receive until you had passed through the valley of the shadow, not of death, although it almost played its part as well. The experience was the means, the catalyst, that brought you the beginning of the realisation of these fundamental, eternal, spiritual truths.

Now you can help others, but do not be disappointed if some are unable to accept what you have to offer. It means they are not ready. When that happens I always say the same thing: shed a silent tear for a lost opportunity.

Just as the way was shown when you needed it, direction will be given in the days that lie ahead.

Rest your faith not only on the knowledge that provides the foundation for your outlook, but also on the fact that you are aware of the tremendous host of enlightened beings in our world who will always come to your aid whenever opportunities for advancing truth are presented to them.

There is nothing to fear. You will rejoice because you will be able to serve, and giving service is most important.

Be grateful for all the opportunities you get for serving others. Have no fear of what the morrow will bring. Difficulties will come, but they are like the clouds that temporarily obscure the sun, which is always there even when you cannot see it. Try to be aware of the strength and light it has to offer.

* * *

"Perhaps you could give me some indication as to how I might better employ my life."

There is always room for improvements. If you were perfect, you would not be in the world of matter.

This question is not easy to answer. Let me put it another way. There is an overruling plan for the whole universe and for all who dwell in it.

This plan unfolds as you begin to realise you are a part of it. It takes time for realisation to dawn. There has to be some crisis, some difficulty, perhaps what is called a tragedy which provides the catalyst for the spirit to become aware of itself. Once that happens, a magnetic link with our world is forged, one that can never be severed.

That has happened in your case, and in the case of everybody in this room. With the realisation comes the desire, or it should happen that way, to fulfil oneself, to use the gifts of the spirit to help others. That is your responsibility as to how you proceed in this direction. Knowledge always brings responsibility.

Correspondingly, however low you have sunk, so equally high can you ascend.

I cannot provide a blueprint for you as to what you can do in the circumstances you find yourself. What I can say is that the way was shown when you needed it most. The way will continue to be shown.

You attract automatically kindred souls in our world whose one desire is to co-operate with you in extending truth, knowledge and power so that you serve others. It is a constantly expanding chain of service as new links are forged in it.

Silver Birch closed the session with these words:

Let us pause to end where we began, with the Great Spirit, the infinite creator, the supreme power that has neither beginning nor end because spirit is eternal and infinite. Let us always seek to help wherever we can. Let us aspire to the highest we can attain so that we imbibe some of its radiance, richness and beauty.

Let us resolve to discover the will of the Great Spirit

and to put it into action. In so doing we achieve
harmony, inner peace, tranquillity, repose and steadfastness. These are important qualities to sustain us and
to inspire us to continue on the work that engages us.
And may the Great Spirit bless you all.

★ ★ ★

*Welcoming a Nigerian Chief, who called him "friend,
philosopher and teacher," the guide asked, "How can I help
you?"*

*The Chief replied: "We may have spiritual ambitions to
benefit ourselves and our fellow men; but living in a material
world we are beset by problems which can delay or hamper
our intention. Can you advise anyone in this position?"*

A similar sort of question was put to the Nazarene.
He replied to the effect, "Render unto Caesar the things
which are Caesar's and unto God the things that are
God's."

Of course you will have problems. Earth is a place
where you are presented with difficulties, frustrations,
obstacles and handicaps. The whole purpose of earthly
existence is to meet conditions that are a challenge to the
evolving spirit so that it can have a chance to express
some of its latent qualities that can be called on in times
of crisis.

You cannot achieve spiritual mastery without con-
quering the problems that you encounter; but none is so
insuperable that you cannot overcome it. You will have
to be patient and pray for guidance that at the right time
the door will open and the way will be shown. I always
tell my friends in very simple language never to bang
against a closed door.

"Is it right to believe only one basic law, of cause and effect,

must operate for all times and in all places? If this is so, why is it that nature, an operation of this law, is either not understood, realised, or blatantly disregarded?"

The law of cause and effect is basic, fundamental and unalterable because you can reap only what you have sown. Effect must follow cause with mathematical accuracy; it cannot be otherwise. In turn the effect becomes the cause by which another effect is set into motion, producing another cause. The process is a constant one. The flower will always be true to its seed.

Throughout the vast variety of the phenomena of nature, everything, small or large, simple or complex, follows the law of cause and effect. None and nothing can interrupt that sequence. If effect did not follow cause, your world, the universe and the vast cosmos would be chaotic. The Great Spirit, God, the Deity, the Supreme Power, would not be the summit of love, wisdom and the perfection of all that exists.

The universe is ruled by divine justice. If at a stroke, by reciting some words said to have religious and spiritual significance, you could obliterate the result of some wrong you have done, then that would be a criticism that the natural law was not perfect in its operation, but unjust because you could change its pattern.

Nature must follow its ordained path, oblivious to man's desire. It has its tasks to perform, and will continue to do so. When man works in harmony with nature he reaps the result. Nature can be profligate in the abundance it has to offer to those who will work in harmony with it.

Whenever man tries to exploit nature, to bend it to his

will, he is attempting to interfere with the infinite processes of creation. The result must be disastrous for him. Man must be blamed for his own folly. Nature will continue to fulfil its ordained purpose.

The law is the law. The law operates with complete impartiality and indifference to man's demands. The buds, the blossom and flowers show themselves as part of the natural law. The law is cause and effect, the sequence that is unalterable.

If you do anything wrong you pay for it. If you do anything good you are the better for it. It is very simple. We bring all the power that we can muster and try to get you always on the path of rectitude. We do not always succeed.

We are dealing with imperfect human beings; there are no perfect ones in your world. Perfection exists only with the Great Spirit. We do not expect you to behave impeccably. We know you will make mistakes. We know you will do the wrong things sometimes because you are human and fallible.

Because we love you we do our best to help you. Sometimes we have to stand aside and let you choose what you will do. At other times, we impress you to the utmost limits of our ability to ensure that you will not do anything wrong which would impede or mar how you must act to fulfil yourselves.

It can be said of the vast majority of people in your world that there is far more goodness than badness, more virtue than vice, more honesty than dishonesty, more service than disservice, more altruism than selfishness.

★ ★ ★

An American couple found disharmony disturbing the peace of their Spiritualist church.

"The circumstances at the moment cannot be overridden. Since we intend moving, perhaps they will change."

How diplomatically conveyed! Did you not hear me say there were no chances, no accidents, no coincidences, no miracles? All is due to the variation of natural law; this is another way of saying that cause and effect are part of an interchangeable sequence.

It is the same pattern. You are led to where you are today. You made the big change in your life when it seemed there was nothing else to be done.

It has brought you to a land which is very familiar to me; there you have found happiness and the opportunity to serve.

Nothing, but nothing, can stop you from rendering the service for which you were born into this world.

The power of the spirit is supreme; there is nothing greater in your world.

Love is the greatest power of all; love is the power of the spirit in operation.

Love, it says in your Bible, is the fulfilling of the law.

You have been very richly blessed, and found in your partner an affinity that you did not think was possible on earth.

The work will always continue; the power of the spirit is here to stay in your world.

Never mind opposition that comes from those who should be its friends and not its foes. I know the problems; they are problems that are human ones.

These are those of development, unfoldment and growth, problems which are inherent in human nature.

You will not always get agreement among those who have our knowledge. Where you cannot find harmony, withdraw. The power of the spirit will still continue to function, to guide and direct you as it has always done.

12: Pilgrims' Progress

Silver Birch always gave words of encouragement to those who help in the Other-Side's plan, whether by their healing or mediumistic gifts, or in the work of publishing evidence of the spirit's survival after bodily death.

Welcoming two editorial staff members of Psychic News, Spiritualism's weekly newspaper founded by his medium in 1932, the guide told them:

★ ★ ★

You cannot measure the results obtained by the printed word.

It is very heartening for us to see how gradually we are achieving a breakthrough in many places where hitherto the truths of the spirit could not be found. From our standpoint your world very largely presents a gloomy, dismal picture. When we come into your environment we are heartened by the lighthouses of the spirit that we see round your globe.

Each is a bridgehead that has been consolidated and fulfils its function in shedding beams that will attract travellers who have lost their spiritual way. We can reach only those who are ready to be reached. We can do nothing with those who are not yet ready to receive either the truths of the spirit or its sublime power.

Where souls are ready, the beam of light will attract them. Gradually they find the path that brings them out of speculation, ignorance and superstition into the expanding light of knowledge and certainty.

You are helping souls to express themselves. You are enabling them to begin to understand the mighty, divine potential they possess.

In many cases they start to exercise it in a manner that will serve others because they are expressing divine gifts that were bestowed on them. Thus the power of the spirit will gradually succeed in infiltrating where before there was barren ground, and that is a cause for rejoicing.

When you get tired and frustrated because you are human and subject to all the weaknesses of humanity, relax and remember you are privileged to be part of a great plan that is taking shape in your world.

The power of the spirit has come to stay. None will be able to drive it away. No church, no synagogue, no chapel, no temple, no priest, no ecclesiastic, no religion will be able to prevent the power of the spirit from continuing to unfold and express itself in your world.

If you succeed in helping only one soul, then all is worth while. Happily we can say there are many who have found truth, that most beauteous of jewels, to have as their permanent possession. And that is the end of a little sermon.

A circle member asked, "Are there no texts?"

Yes, my text is, "God is love." It is because we love you that we come back to your world, which has very little to attract us compared with what is available in our world.

We love you because we see in you channels that can be used by the divine power to serve others. There are millions who need the service that only the power of the spirit can provide.

The religions of your world as propounded today have lost their way. They flounder in sterility and barrenness. They are embroiled in theology, creeds, dogmas, doctrines, rites and ceremonies that are only the trappings. The reality is the power of the spirit, the vivifying force that alone brings life wherever it can manifest.

We are getting further than you can realise.

I regard it as a privilege to have worked so long in your world. I look back and see the tremendous progress that has been made. It is a cause for rejoicing.

There is no other form of organisation, and no other individual, unless they are endowed with these powers, able to act in this unique way as channels of the Great Spirit. There are many sincere persons doing the best they can, but unless they are filled with the power of the spirit they are as little children groping in the dark.

If there have been mistakes, as there have been; if there has been delay, as there has been; if there has been separation when there should be unity, shed a tear for those who had the chance and did not take it. Seeds have been sown; some will bear fruit. We have to contend with the personal problems of human beings, with those who think that the attainment of official position is more important than the spread of divine truths.

That is why I have said the angels sometimes weep. There can be some excuse for those who are ignorant. What excuse can there be for those who have the knowledge and put self before service to others? But the work will go on. We are here to stay; we are not passengers; we are not transient; we are permanent.

We are here to teach people of your world how to save themselves by their own efforts, with the knowledge of who and what they are, what they can do to banish hatred and division, to realise that though there may be differences of colour, caste, creed and nationality, they are all one in spirit and that unity of the spirit is stronger than all the differences that divide them.

We will win through; we will not retreat. There may be delays or hindrances, but we cannot be swept away, no matter what churches, popes, prelates, archbishops, rabbis or ministers may say. It is they who have lost their way.

We are, like John the Baptist, preparing the way for the world that is to be, where peace, harmony, love, compassion, co-operation and concord reign, where violence is forgotten and all strive to serve and help one another, and transform the earth into the kingdom of heaven that it can and will be.

You are aware of the great power that enfolds and guides you and of the love that comes from our world which acts as a shield at all times.

You are helping people far more than you realise. You cannot measure the results that follow. The printed word is very important. Now there is my spoken word which I am told adds its helpfulness to the printed one.

Together we form part of the vast army of the spirit which is engaged in a very important campaign. It is to try and lessen the evils of your world, banishing some of its darkness, to bring more love into it, more compassion for one another and for all the animals who share the planet with you.

We rejoice at what together we have achieved and we await with confidence the tasks that are still to be performed in helping souls to attain freedom and liberation, so that they too can make their contribution to the world in which they dwell.

Our numbers are small relatively speaking, but the power behind us is the mightiest in the universe. None can gainsay it, none can overthrow it, none can prevent it from operation. There are no bodies or organisations that can in any way prevent the power of the spirit from its directed plan of bringing enlightenment to the people of your world.

I have only just returned from the higher spheres which are my natural habitat. I have sought refreshment and renewal in higher spheres than the one I usually occupy when I communicate with you according to the manner of your world.

I have taken counsel with the wise ones who are part of the hierarchy charged with the vital task of ensuring that the will of the Great Spirit must prevail.

It is heartening to be told of the spiritual advances that have been and will be made.

As a result I return to resume the very important task on which we are all engaged. It is to demonstrate the supremacy of the spirit and all its accompanying gifts so that your world may become richer in beauty and grandeur. Gradually it will rid itself of the greed, selfishness, disruption, violence and all that prevents it from being the kingdom of heaven upon earth.

When we come back to this dreary, dismal world of yours, where there is so much apprehension of what the morrow will bring, we can say that fear should be abandoned because the light of the spirit is gradually brightening and its power infiltrating everywhere.

Those who are privileged to have a knowledge of spiritual realities should never allow any kind of degree of pessimism to effect a lodgment within their beings. The power of the spirit is greater than any force that humans can command. Man can delay; man can hinder; man can impede. But he cannot prevent the descent of the mighty power of the spirit to fulfil its ordained plan.

We have established bridgeheads in as many lands as we can, and they are there to stay.

These include lighthouses of the spirit that constantly revolve, shedding a beam for those who have lost their way. They will come to you and to others because you are privileged to be channels for the greatest power in the universe.

I wish I had the language to convey the tremendous strength, vitality, force and energy involved in the power of the spirit. There are no words to enable you to comprehend it. What you are receiving today is only an infinitesimal part of what can be transmitted.

Spirit power is infinite. The amount that you receive depends on the stage of evolution you have reached. Increase your receptivity, and even more of the sublime power will stream through you to work its wonders, its beauty, its solace, its healing.

Silver Birch advised a journalist who had returned to Britain after an unsuccessful emigration to Germany:

You are in your world to learn lessons. Many are learned when you make what you call wrong decisions and fall by the wayside. I am not sure than in doing so you fall flat on your face.

You will survive; the way will be shown.

"I wanted to revisit a country I had known for years. You cannot bathe always in the same river. The work I do was not forthcoming. I learned that you can have great comfort, be in a pleasant place and still be miserable."

The trouble is that with your knowledge you cannot live in a spiritual desert. And in deserts oases are very hard to find. But the situation is not irreparable. You have been involved in far more difficult conditions than the ones which prevail today. Then you were guided and brought safely through. A place was found for you where you could unfold in a freedom that had not been possible.

Lift up your heart, do not worry and have no fear. Fear is a bad counsellor. Fear always impedes the channel through which help can come from our world. Be confident; know that the way will be shown. You will look back and say, "I am not sorry because I have added to my mental and spiritual equipment in what I have learned."

"I have learned a great deal."

I always tell my friends that you begin by adding knowledge to faith and you end by adding faith to knowledge. It is not possible in your world or in mine to possess all the knowledge that exists. Knowledge, like the Great Spirit, is infinite and you will constantly be adding to your store of it.

So hold your head high; look forward, not backward. The pages of the past have been turned; they cannot be turned again. There are always fresh pages in the book of life waiting for you to turn them. Live for the day, not yesterday. It is today that you will sow the seeds of a harvest that you will reap on the morrow.

"Through going away I have got out of the stream that I was very well in. It is difficult to get back. Are there ways for me to find the work I want to do, which is the spreading of our knowledge to help other people?"

You have more work to do than you can accomplish. I have said this before and will say it again. Even people in your world who have knowledge of spiritual realities sometimes fail to realise that we can do things only in our way and in our time. We cannot do them in your way and in your time. To influence your world we have to exert very subtle and delicate influences, vibrations that require the most complex manipulation.

Often your impatience, because people in your world are always in a hurry, can delay the results because you do not provide the conditions which make it easier for them to occur. What we ask of you is the ability to be receptive, confident, tranquil, serene, to know beyond doubt that what is best for you in all aspects will be achieved, but only when the time is ripe. Hold on to that.

Do not be impatient. The trouble with your world is that people are in such a hurry.

Have you any idea how long it took us to get you to wake? Things of the spirit cannot be accelerated. They have to follow laws which infinite wisdom devised. I repeat myself, but truth is worth repeating. We can do things only in our way and in our time. We cannot do them in your way and in your time.

You are not the best judges of what is good for you spiritually. Sometimes if your prayers were answered you would be spiritually worse as a result. We will help you, guide you, never fail you or forsake you. We will not desert you.

We have given evidence of the mighty power of the spirit and what it can accomplish in your world. Those of you who have trod this path with us know what spirit power has accomplished. We all have work to do in your world. It is a great work. We may be few in number, but the task is assigned to us by higher beings.

They are charged with the duty of ensuring that the power of the spirit shall continue to prevail in your world so that its benign influence will be made available to millions of people.

There are too many souls in your world living in darkness, doubt, dismay and despair. We have to reach them. We have to show them the love of the Great Spirit. We have to make them accessible to that mighty power that can regenerate them and enable them to have a rich, full, self-fulfilling life.

At all times we are breaking through and establishing bridgeheads in new territories. Rejoice at what has been accomplished and know that even more will be done with your help.

The easy tasks are not for those with knowledge. The more knowledge you have the more difficulties you must expect. I am not going to be popular for saying this.

Some difficulties you must expect as challenges to be welcomed and overcome, so that you can allow latent powers to rise to the surface. If those with knowledge were given the easiest tasks it would make a mockery of divine justice. So when you meet difficulty do not despair. Treat it as the challenge which it is, knowing that within you and without there is the power that will enable you to succeed.

The work on which we are all engaged is very important. Though we are few in numbers, the power behind us is mighty. As it gradually reveals itself to more and more people in your world, it fulfils its appointed role in the divine plan.

You cannot measure what is being accomplished. There are no instruments capable of registering it. Souls are being touched, minds are being opened.

There was a teacher in your world who said, "The child is the repository of infinite possibility." You all possess infinite possibilities. In your world you register only a tiny fragment of what you could achieve if you were able to attune yourselves to higher spheres and levels of attainment and thus become the recipients of greater power.

I teach a gospel of optimism based on knowledge. I see no grounds for pessimism for those who have knowledge. All your lives have a purpose. The natural laws do not work by chance, coincidence or even miracles. They operate as immutable laws which have always been in existence, requiring no revision or repeal of any kind.

The Great Spirit is perfect. There can be nothing higher than infinite wisdom and infinite love. These are accessible to you, but not in their fullness. The more you increase your capacity to receive the more you can receive, and the larger, grander and nobler your lives will become.

What we have to offer are sublime truths based on eternal realities. The Great Spirit will not fail; the natural laws will continue to operate. If perils seem to be coming your way, whatever problems you may encounter, you have within you the power to overcome them. And you have access to the greater power that comes from above, on which you can call.

When trouble looms, as inevitably it must, withdraw from your world, with all its strident clangour, into the silence of meditation. Let your soul begin to become far more aware, so that you the spirit can absorb the radiance that is around and about you. I have not said anything new because in truth there is nothing new to be said. There are only ways in which you can express eternal truth.

★　★　★

"In indecision should one wait for guidance, or use free will? Sometimes one has to make a big decision. Then one does not know whether to charge in or whether to wait for events to show the way. This is sometimes difficult."

Never bang on a closed door; wait for it to open. There is a plan, not only for the universe but for every individual within it. The plan will operate. I have told my friends here many, many times that we can only do things in our way and in our time. We cannot do them in your way and in your time.

One reason is that you are not the best judges of what is right for you. We from our vantage point consider we are better judges of what is right for you materially, mentally and spiritually. Wait, and the door will open. It has opened for you many times.

13: Healing – The Second Chance

Spiritual healing, either by laying-on of hands or by mental contact over scores or thousands of miles, is a valuable part of the Other-Side plan.

Millions of sufferers, dismissed as medically incurable by hospitals and doctors, have found relief or permanent cures through healing mediums who channel divine power, sometimes being entranced, sometimes linking mentally with their spirit guides. These guides are often former surgeons or doctors still desiring to serve ailing humanity.

Always the aim is to touch the sick person's soul, awakening it to awareness of spiritual realities.

★   ★   ★

The Great Spirit, with infinite wisdom and love, provides sufferers with a second chance when the people of the medical world say no more can be done.

What is important is to touch souls. Then the power of the spirit can quicken the flicker of divinity into a beauteous, lambent flame, so that the majesty of latent divinity shines through, enabling their bodies to become well, their minds to learn the lesson and their spiritual natures to unfold further as a result.

If a soul is touched because of the healing, then gratitude should be given to the Great Spirit for the

111

privilege of the service the healer has rendered.

If a soul is not touched though the healing has cured the physical body, that is very sad. It means the sufferer has been given the opportunity of attaining awareness and unfortunately has failed to take it. A healer must do the best he can, and allow the fullest amount of spirit power to pour through and work its divine will wherever it possibly can.

Not all souls can be receptive because that is not possible. A healer cannot cure everybody who comes to him. If you can obtain results with the hopeless cases, then that should be the clearest evidence to any with the ability to think and reason that a power vastly superior to matter has been at work.

The healing power, which is divine in origin and in essence, is among the most important forces streaming into your world today. It is a very sick world. There are increasing numbers of diseases caused by the stresses and strains of the inharmonious conditions in which too many people live. Your so-called civilisation has divorced man from nature which provides some of the sources of his energy.

Then the human battery, the soul, is depleted and has to be recharged by the power of the spirit. When that happens and the battery is working, then you achieve health, which is harmony between body, mind and spirit. The Great Spirit with infinite wisdom has created the human frame and all its concomitant parts in such a fashion that the spirit contains self-healing properties.

You get disease when the natural unity between man's triple nature of body, mind and spirit are out of harmony. Health is wholeness.

What happens when you become the channel as a healer? The life force, that is, the power of the spirit, pours through you and makes contact with the soul of the patient to charge that battery and establish the harmony which has been disrupted by whatever conditions caused the disease.

The essence of all healing is that the healer should have suffered and have compassion for the sufferers who come to him. It is the only way that the laws work. I, who have lived much longer than any of you, continue to marvel at the infinite wisdom of the Great Spirit that devised the universal laws to ensure that everything comes within their operation.

It is in the storm you appreciate peace, in the rain that you appreciate the sunshine. It is the law of polarity at work the whole time. If all were light you would not appreciate the light. It is the contrast, the comparison, that always enables you to differentiate and to appreciate the wondrous operation of natural law.

So you suffer, and in your suffering, your spirit begins to come into its own. As a result you are able to unfold your healing gift and know what others feel when they come to you to be healed.

I always say to any of the instruments of the spirit whom I welcome here, have no fear for the morrow. Those you can help will be brought to you. You do not have to go out and proclaim, "I am a healer, who wants healing?" This is not the way that the spirit works.

If you succeed in ending only physical aches and diseases, that is good. But it is better if, in addition, they realise the implication of what is happening. Their spirit starts to come into its own and they begin to fulfil themselves and to achieve the purpose for which they incarnated into your world.

That is the important part. The physical results are good if you achieve them; better still if awareness of spiritual realities follows.

* * *

"Why are some patients healed and others cannot be?"

Because some are ready to be healed spiritually and others are not. But the acid test is not whether the body is healed, but whether the soul is touched.

A circle member who is a healer asked: "There are obvious cases where some people who come for healing are ill because they have broken the law. They receive healing and then become just as bad because they continue to break the law. Is it part of the plan that healing should be given again and again?"

What we must do is to help souls who come to us. What they do afterwards is their responsibility. If only the body is made well, then the healing has failed. It is the soul which must be touched and quickened into activity.

If they have not learned as a result of the healing the implications as to how they should order their lives, then that must be accounted a failure. They should realise that the power that has been at work is intended not only to heal bodies, but to heal minds so that there is an understanding of what life is all about. It takes time.

"Should a healer be concerned with the same thing time and time again if necessary?"

You must not be in a position where you refuse to help. A soul asks for help, and it is no part of the healer's province to lay down laws as to how it should be given. The healer's task is to heal. If the sufferer's soul is touched, enlightenment will come. If it is not touched, then at least you have made a body better than it was before, even if only for a short time.

You must do the best you can and never refuse help when it is sought. The healer must be available. If a recipient misbehaves later and induces more difficulties, that is his responsibility.

All souls can be touched, because the soul is the portion of the Great Spirit, the divinity that is within them. Being infinite, it is capable of infinite development. That is elementary logic.

As to what constitutes readiness, the answer is the gold that can only be found after it has gone through the process of eliminating the dross.

If earthly life was a monotone, if there was only light and no darkness, joy and no pain, food and no hunger, you would not appreciate its value. It is life's polarity that brings you an understanding of its purpose and possibilities. Love and hate are equal and opposite. Hate can be transformed into love, just as love can be transformed into hate. The soul can come into its own only when it has emerged as steel does from the furnace, the gold from the dross, the diamond from the ore. Otherwise there is no means by which the soul can be quickened into activity in your world.

Pain and suffering are regarded as miseries; they are not. They have divine parts to play in the evolution of the individual. What you have to do is to help those who are brought to you. If it is an evolved person, try to comfort the individual with the evidence that can be obtained about the reality of the afterlife, that love, like life, continues to survive.

If it is a sick person the healing is the demonstration of a power at work for which there is no material explanation. If it is someone who has lost his way, guidance can be provided.

All you can hope to do is to provide the catalyst that will produce the result. If you succeed, then you have helped an individual to find himself. That should make your heart rejoice. If you have failed, then it is not your fault. It means the individual has had the opportunity, but is not ready to take it.

"Leaving aside the people who for some reason of their own do not want to be healed and therefore cannot be, or I think they cannot be, where does karma come into this picture? Some people are receptive and are receiving the healing, but are not cured. Is this because of some karmic condition, or some failure on the part of the healer?"

This is a very complex question because there is no single explanation for what happens when healing is demonstrated. The object of all spiritual healing is to touch the sufferer's soul. You began by referring to the diseases that have their origin in the mind and which the word psychosomatic explains. The physical ailment, in the vast majority of cases, is only the outward expression of an inner disharmony.

Your world is seeing so many illnesses and diseases which are the result of tensions, strains and frustrations to which people are subjected. There are very few, if any, diseases which are purely physical in their origin.

Spiritual healing utilises a divine power which emanates from the supreme creator. Its quality, quantity and nature depend on the development of the healer as to the amount and type that can be registered through him or

her. And this is determined by the prevailing conditions, and also by the mental and physical conditions
of the healer and the patient.

The healing will succeed only when the patient is
spiritually ready, and touched, because then there is the
quickening of the soul. Otherwise it is a purely physical
reflex action. Success may be temporary or permanent,
but what is vital is the effect on the patient's spiritual
nature.

The object of all earthly existence is that the human
spirit, the divine element in all mankind and animals,
and indeed in all life, is to be quickened so that what is
only a spark can become a flickering light, and gradually
a beauteous flame. Self-fulfilment begins, and people in
your world are able to enjoy what life, not only on its
surface but in its more important inner aspect, has to
offer them.

You introduced the question of karma, the law of
cause and effect, sowing and reaping, which operates in
all worlds and at all times. Sometimes you have a
patient with a karmic condition which is a carry-over
from a previous existence. If the karmic condition has
not outworked itself, the healing will appear to be a
failure. If the patient has reached that stage in spiritual
development where the effect has completely followed
the cause and there is no more karma to manifest, the
healing will be successful because the soul is ready.

*"You have often said, 'If the mind is right the body will be
right.' Yet most mediums seem to suffer ill-health or some
disability. Surely they would have minds that are 'right.' If
suffering in this life is due to karma, how does this agree with
your statement?"*

Mediums cannot be exempt from natural law, which encompasses all without exception and without deviation. If there is ill-health there are two reasons.

One is that there is not the harmony between spirit, mind and body which produces the wholeness that is health. The other possibility is a karmic condition, which means that the soul has yet to achieve progress on earth that cannot be attained elsewhere because of what has happened in a previous existence.

In an ideal world mediums would be ideal people, but you are not living in an ideal world.

"You say the object of healing is to touch the soul of the patient, and succeeds when the spirit and the mind are right. How does this apply with babies and animals?"

It still applies. The spirit must be right to help the conditions. The baby's soul has to be touched, and so has the soul of the animal. I do not see the difficulty. But I was speaking generally about those who come for healing and have gone a long way in their earthly sojourn. Healing is a complex subject. In its simplest form it is from spirit, through spirit, to spirit. It is from the Great Spirit, by way of the healer's spirit, to the patient's spirit.

Now when you come to babies and animals you have not the same spiritual considerations involved. It is usually only the spiritual condition to be corrected. Even so, that can be done only spiritually, not physically. The soul has to be charged so that it eliminates the blockage preventing the harmony between mind, spirit and body, the only means for health to function. Sometimes in the case of babies – I will not now pursue this – there are karmic problems involved.

"*I understand that one can call upon the God-presence within oneself to heal. You have just said that spirit healing comes from spirit through spirit to spirit and the soul within is charged. This seems to me an outside influence if it comes from the Great Spirit.*"

If you are calling upon your inner core to achieve healing, that is not true spiritual healing. It is more in the realm of what could be described as magnetic healing. True spiritual healing involves the transmission of spirit power which emanates from the Great Spirit. The Great Spirit is the source, the power house, the reservoir, the storehouse. That is what spiritual healing means.

"*We are all part of that Great Spirit, we are all divine.*"

Yes, you are the Great Spirit in miniature certainly, but the potency that you have within you is minute compared with the infinite power that emanates from the Great Spirit. Self-healing requires attunement and receptivity, a combination of getting the inner power to work and to be accessible to the outer power that flows from the Great Spirit and can come through you at the same time.

"*Would you say that it was a good idea to promote this form of healing so that people are not dependent on others?*"

This is not an easy question, for it depends on the person's knowledge.

Your function is to be a channel for the healing power. If the patient is spiritually ready, the results will come. If the soul is touched, then the healing is successful. If only the physical body gets better, the goal has not been achieved. The object is to bring spiritual awareness.

"All doctors treat the physical body, but some people try to heal the etheric body. Is that possible?"

All true spiritual healing works in a very simple fashion. You are a spirit with a body, and not a body with a spirit. When your body is ill or diseased and suffers as a result, it is due to the simple fact that harmony, wholeness which ensures health, no longer obtains.

Not only are you spirit and body, you are also mind, the means through which the spirit registers itself and allows the body to function. In spiritual healing, the power of the spirit, which emanates from its divine source, is transmitted to a healer who has the gift of healing, which is a spiritual one. Through him the power is directed to the spirit of the sufferer.

The whole exercise is a spiritual one. The spirit, being the life force, will try to produce harmony where there was disharmony. This is some blockage, some interference, which means that the three aspects of mind, spirit and body are not working efficiently. When it succeeds, then wholeness, which is health, is restored to the patient.

Whether this is done through the etheric, the spirit or the astral body or not is a matter only of technique. What must happen is that the power of the spirit should recharge the spirit of the patient so that it can attain its true potential and enable harmony to be restored.

★　★　★

"Can you say something about emotions? We let them rule us. So many things which we think are good, patriotism and some love which can be a form of selfishness, are not good."

The motive is the all-important qualification. If

patriotism means only love of one's country and the people who dwell in it, and there is no wish to extend that love to other countries and other people, then that is a form of selfishness.

The supreme guiding principle is love which expresses itself in service, compassion, humility, tolerance and co-operation, seeking harmony wherever it can. Love is the greatest power in the universe.

You are human beings. You are not perfect; you will never attain perfection in your world, or even in mine. You are developing, evolving, growing beings. You have the divine potential. You are endowed with a measure of free will.

You can, if you like, behave in accordance with the divine image with which you are created, and allow the qualities of divinity to be expressed. Or you have the choice of allowing the lower passions and emotions to direct your lives and to be merely selfish in your desire for acquiring the material things which can never be your eternal possessions.

That is the choice which the Great Spirit allows to every one of the children of earth. But being human, you make mistakes; you fall by the wayside.

Our judgement is based on the motive. Moreover the Great Spirit has endowed everyone with an infallible monitor known as the conscience, which always unerringly shows whether your action is right or wrong.

"I have known so many people who have suffered depression. Is there anything that we can do to help?"

They have to learn to change their outlook and to have a faith built on the foundation of knowledge. Faith built on credulity will easily vanish because it is based on shifting sands. Faith founded on knowledge will endure.

All of you are privileged to have seen what the power of the spirit can do. You are aware there is a highly intelligent plan devised by the Infinite Power. That plan embraces each one of you. It should give you a constant hopefulness, an optimism, a radiant knowledge in which the darkness of depression or fear should never engulf you.

★ ★ ★

Silver Birch told circle members suffering from minor winter ailments:

I always try to warn you when I see the danger signals. I am sorry when you fall by the wayside because my words are ignored. The supreme teaching we offer is personal responsibility.

Again and again I would have tried, if I were allowed, to shoulder your problems. But I know I must not do so because you have to find your spiritual way by what you do.

This is the season when you must exercise the greatest care and not overtax the machinery that is your physical body. Rest is essential. It is rest you need because without it you impair the mechanism by which the spirit can function in your world.

I do not say this in any harsh tone, because I love you. But I would be failing in my duty if I did not point to the inexorable laws on which the whole of life is founded.

★ ★ ★

"The demands for her services as a translator had resulted in

*overwork "because I have had to meet deadlines," said one old
friend.*

I find it very amusing that you should speak to me
about deadlines. I did not make your world, neither did
I create the bodies of those who dwell in it. All I know is
that your bodies are remarkable and complex forms of
machinery. The result is the creation of something
which even the most qualified engineers in your world
cannot construct.

Here are millions of cells of blood, sinew, nerves,
tissue, and a whole collection of minerals all ceaselessly
at work day and night to ensure that you should be
efficient so that the spirit can be expressed properly.

The physical body seems to be the only machine in
your world that never gets any rest or overhaul. If you
tax it too much, it has to call a halt because some part of
it becomes defective through over-use. I am not responsible for that.

If the Great Spirit wanted you to be perfect in your
world you would have had perfect bodies. But your
world is merely one of many you will inhabit as part of
eternal evolution. And so you are responsible for maintaining your body. If you overwork it, it will not
function as it should.

I say the same thing to another person here. She says
there are problems and difficulties. But then I reply: "I
know. If there were no problems and difficulties you
would not be where you are, because you are on earth to
deal with them."

There are challenges which you have to meet because
in doing so you call on your reservoir, your potential,
some of the latent divinity to help you. But do not

overtax the body. Give it rest when it says, "I am tired, I cannot do any more."

As much as we love you, we cannot live your lives for you. We can guide you; we can help you; we can sustain you; we can point the way; but we cannot assume your responsibilities. We will never fail. We will do whatever lies in our power to ensure that you receive protection when it is necessary, but you are responsible for what you do.

★   ★   ★

Surgeons are devoting their skills to transplanting corneas, kidneys and even hearts of the newly dead to replace diseased organs in the living.

Silver Birch gave his views on this controversial subject when he was asked:

"Are you against the transplant of corneas? Surely there is nothing spiritually wrong about that?"

As a principle I am opposed to transplants. I don't question the sincerity of the motive of those who offer bodily parts to be used in the service of others.

The Great Spirit has endowed every human with a physical body to express the spirit that is responsible for its life.

This is an intimate relationship between the body and the spirit. If it were necessary for transplants then you would not have the failures when hearts and kidneys are transplanted into other bodies.

The question of corneas is very difficult. I don't want it to appear that I am indifferent to suffering. But sometimes there is a karmic condition involved. I know this can be regarded as the easy way out of the problem, yet nothing happens by chance in your world or in mine. The law is supreme and regulates everything.

Where there is blindness it is a result of cause and effect. Whether it is spiritually better for the blind person to have sight is a matter that could be debated for a very long time.

Physically there could be a benefit, but not necessarily a spiritual one. I, from my vantage point, can stress only the spiritual aspect as the one that is the most important.

"Would you apply that principle to ordinary illnesses?"

Only if it is a karmic condition. Then the healing will not succeed, and similarly the cornea will not produce sight.

"But if transplants were not meant to be used, people would not be able to do operations."

You have free will. You are not puppets. You can take the road to the right or to the left: you have a choice. If the Great Spirit wanted you to be merely marionettes you would have been created that way.

You have within you the power to help what I call the infinite processes of creation. Similarly you have the power to delay, to hinder, to hamper; but you cannot alter them.

"It could well be spiritually wrong to develop along a road of science whereby ordinary human beings are patched from one another. Everybody has a spiritual basis."

That is the purpose of our teaching. The body is important because it is the temple of the spirit. If, because one has in some way transgressed the natural law, an illness results, you must pay the price for it; you cannot avoid it.

I am not opposed to the surgeons' work. I am not against skin grafting. I am not against any sincere motive to serve. But I can approach all the problems involved only from the view-point of the underlying spiritual motivation.

14: The Healing Mission

A healer's life, though spiritually rewarding, is never easy. Silver Birch always encourages those who use their gifts to help others.

★ ★ ★

I love all those who try to serve, whether it be with healing or any other form of mediumship. I love them all, for I know the difficulties they will encounter because that is an integral part of their mission. In the case of a healer, you have to suffer in order to have the essential compassion for sufferers to come to you. It is only when you have plumbed the depths yourself that you have the rightful feeling for others who turn to you when there is nowhere else to go.

You are richly blessed. I cannot say to instruments of the spirit that their lives will be beds of roses. That is not the way spiritual mastery is obtained. The higher you seek to rise, the more difficult it must become. On that road you tread it becomes lonelier as gradually the familiar landmarks must be left behind.

If the prizes of the spirit were easily gained, they would not be worth the having. Achievement, attainment, these mean sacrifices. But there is a law of compensation. Whatever you have lost materially will be restored and replenished with far more than has been lost. We will always ensure that your material necessities will be forthcoming. We cannot promise you so-called luxuries of earth-life; many of them are far from luxurious in the effect that they have. What we can promise is that as you serve, so will you be served.

It is not the curing of the physical body that is the most important. It is touching the soul of the sufferer to increase the divine spark, thus ensuring, as far as you can, that the result of the healing will bring awareness and understanding of eternal spiritual realities for the one who has had the illness, so that it becomes a catalyst. That is what matters.

If you heal a body and do not touch the soul, then from our viewpoint the healing is a failure. If you touch the soul, you help to fan the divine spark. You help to achieve a closer unity between the individual and the great sublime supreme power that endowed that person with life. That is important.

No others in your world can perform that task except those endowed with the gifts of the spirit. It cannot be easy, it must be difficult; but you will not be presented with any obstacle or hurdle for which the power will not be provided so that you will overcome it. Once you consent to serve, the way is shown. There is nothing to fear for what the morrow will bring forth.

You cannot help all who come to you, but your availability is a means by which they can find their true self. If you succeed, then express your gratitude to the Great Spirit. If you fail, the failure is not yours. The patient has had an opportunity and has not taken it. You are the recipient of a divine power. Expressing it brings a great responsibility to do the best you can.

The laying on of hands is merely playing with the

toys. What is important is to bring awareness, realisation, to touch the soul, I cannot put it clearer than that. Every individual in your world is a combination of physical body, mind and spirit. These are the three aspects of the one total self. They are not divisible, but essential parts of the one whole.

If you touch the soul, then you help the other components of body and mind to achieve the wholeness that brings health. So let them play their respective parts and bring health, certainty, confidence, inner well-being, awareness, so that they are at peace with themselves and with everybody else they encounter.

We are concerned with touching souls so that the spark of the divine spirit which is embedded within every human being can be fanned and become a beauteous flame. Thus the divinity within finds a fuller, richer, more majestic expression.

Your world is full of millions of people who do not know what they are there for, who they are, what it is that they must achieve whilst they are incarnate on earth. You can help them to realise that they are spirits with bodies, that the real individual is the deathless spirit, that the spirit is there to gain the experience to equip it for its larger life in our world. That is the most important thing that you can do.

You demonstrate that the Great Spirit, the apex of love and wisdom and compassion, provides everyone with the opportunity to find himself or herself and begin to live, as all people in your world should live, not in superstition, ignorance or darkness, but in the full light of knowledge, with serenity and confidence as their constant companions.

You are not responsible for what others do or say. You are responsible only for what you do or say. Do not concern yourself with the opinions or actions of others.

If you are hurt, it seems that there is still some room for development. Do not allow any thoughts of any kind from any source to hinder, mar or delay the service that you can render. You have been endowed with a gift. Use it wherever you can.

You have heard about the angels weeping? They weep often when they see those who are not behaving in a fashion that is consistent with their knowledge and understanding. But we realise they are not perfect because they are human. You will all make mistakes. There is a divine purpose and plan for all of us.

You feel lonely. Every soul treading the path of attainment must experience loneliness. But you have the companionship of evolved beings who will never desert you. Your strength comes not from your world but from ours. The source of all your inspiration is in our realm.

We will not forget you. We will not leave you. We will not let you down. We will always encourage you to do the best you can.

Help wherever opportunity arises, and know that you are fulfilling yourself, which is the purpose of your being on earth.

It is only human to have doubts. Do not worry. Worry disturbs the conditions and makes it even more difficult. Have faith, founded on the priceless knowledge which is yours. That knowledge is incontrovertible. It provides the solid, enduring foundation on which to build the whole of your life.

If doubt enters your mind, as it will do, then think back to the past, to the days of darkness and difficulty when there seemed no road to tread, where none was able to offer help, when it seemed that you had come to the end of everything that life could offer.

Then in the darkness and gloom the little light of the spirit began to show its way to bring you where you are today.

You have many more pages of your earthly book to be turned. Thank the Great Spirit for the opportunities of service provided for you.

★　★　★

Silver Birch told an Australian healer and his wife: Not only have you travelled a long way physically, but similarly it has been a long journey spiritually to bring you where you now are.

Like all those who are instruments of the spirit it has not been an easy road for you.

In order to become ambassadors for the Great Spirit, the human channels have to be tried and tested so that their latent strength can rise to the surface. They are then ready to meet the challenges that their mission will inevitably make them encounter.

It is not possible to achieve even the first steps in spiritual mastery unless you are ready to do so by a process which means that you must suffer.

Suffering is the crucible. Those on whom the Great Spirit with infinite wisdom has bestowed the gift of healing must experience difficulty, sorrow, crisis and trial so that they can have compassion for the ones who will come to them in their suffering and ask for healing.

But there is a law of compensation. As low as you sink materially, so correspondingly can you rise spiritually.

The story of every potential healer and medium follows a similar pattern. They reach that stage when they feel that nothing materially offers any hope. It is then that the soul becomes ready to receive the influx of power and inspiration which will enable the owner to begin to fulfil himself or herself.

Spiritual growth is not achieved when the sun is shining and the sky is cloudless. It is when the storm is blowing, the wind raging and all looks dark, gloomy and depressing, that the soul begins to come into its own and the way is shown for what lies ahead.

The law of compensation is automatic in its operation. No matter how much your soul has cried out for help and guidance when none seemed possible, you get the richness of the reward in being able to serve others as you were served and the way was shown to you. That is what I tell all healers and mediums.

You two are giving a unique service in your part of the world. You should rejoice at the opportunities to fulfil yourselves and also show that the Great Spirit provides every one of His children with a second chance. When doctors, despite their skills, learning and experience, say they can do no more, the power of the spirit can often produce results which bring health where it was absent.

You will not be able to do this for everybody who comes to you. It is not possible to cure every sufferer who knocks at your door. Some are not ready; others have to endure their illness because it is a karmic condition which has its part to play in their lives.

Silver Birch then asked the healer:

What made you decide to practise healing?

"A need within to see if I could be an instrument for the spirit world to bring about improvement in people's physical and spiritual condition."

Did you find that it worked?

"Yes."

It says in your Bible, "Add to your faith knowledge." I have to tell you, as I have said to others, that to your knowledge you must add faith. The difference is quite simple. It is not a play on words. When you have no knowledge it is good to have faith; not blind, credulous, unreasonable faith.

Because you are human beings in an imperfect world, it is impossible for you to have all the knowledge that there is, because knowledge, like the Great Spirit, is infinite. As you become more receptive you are able to receive greater knowledge. As you develop, more spirit power can flow through you.

So, because of the knowledge you have, treat that as the foundation on which to order your lives, and have faith that the way will be shown what it is you have to do. To this I will add something else.

Before you came into your world this is what you chose to do. It took some time before awareness came. The whole plan was revealed to you before you incarnated. That plan, if you co-operate and are patient, will fulfil itself.

Do not be in a hurry. The things of the spirit cannot be accelerated beyond their natural growth. You can have instant coffee, but you cannot have instant spiritual attainment. It is a slow, steady, but sure process that is achieved only one step at a time. I marvel at the perfection of the natural laws and the way in which they operate.

I have asked you one question and will ask you another. Why did you want to come to this gathering tonight?

"Because we have read of your teachings. When newcomers are brought into our environment we suggest that to the many questions they have they will find the answers if they read the books that contain your teaching. Because we were coming over from Australia we thought it would be a privilege to meet you."

Turning to the stenographer the guide calls his scribe, Silver Birch said: Do you hear that? Without her you would not have these books containing the teaching given to me so that I can transmit it to you.

It is always a great joy to welcome here any channel of the spirit. If there is anything I can do to help them in their ministry, it is a privilege. It is one of the reasons why I have returned to your world to help wherever I can.

Here the healer's wife said: "At the present time I am trying to spread spirit teachings. I seem to have been going through a schooling process, but not specialising in any particular aspect. Is it possible for the spirit world to inform me into which channel I will be directed?"

Do not worry, the way will be shown. Just follow your intuition and the inspiration that comes. If there are any doubts at any time, withdraw into the silence, meditate, and you will find the answers come to you.

You are doing very, very well. You are making your

mark in a vast continent where these truths are sorely needed.

People are coming to you. Do not go looking for them. Just be available. They will continue to come to you because they will have heard what the power of the spirit has done for others. If you help them, rejoice. If you cannot help them, shed a silent tear that they had their chance and could not take it.

"If a person is in poor health should he or she stop healing for the moment?"

No. Only unless they are in such a pitiable condition it makes it impossible for the power of the spirit to operate.

There are many excellent healers who suffer from poor health because they are transmitters; as long as they have the ability to transmit they will have the power flow through them.

★　★　★

Welcoming a healer and his wife, Silver Birch said to the husband:

The last time we met you had many grounds for criticism about the problems, difficulties, hindrances and frustrations which seemed to be troubling you. I hope that position has been changed.

"There is an improvement. I am learning to live with it."

The whole of earthly life consists of learning to live with it, facing up to the problems that come your way, overcoming them as best you can, and awaiting the next one. They are challenges you have to meet so that the real you, the spirit, can evolve, develop and unfold as a result, and emerge better and stronger because of what you have achieved.

It would be folly to tell any disciple who seeks greater truth and understanding that the path will be an easy one. Spiritual mastery is slowly attained. The prizes of the spirit are not quickly earned. But once they are in your possession they are there for all time. They will never be lost, which is something that can never be said for your material possessions.

You both are the recipients of more guidance than you can appreciate. If you were clairvoyant you would be aware of the great love that surrounds you and ensures that no real harm can ever befall you. So every morning await with eager anticipation the spiritual adventures that will unfold for you. And, as I often tell my friends, look back and see how the signposts of the spirit pointed the way for you, and guidance came even when it appeared you were in the blackness of despair. Is that right?"

The answer was, "Yes. It has given me strength."

To endure the suffering?

"Yes."

There is no suffering so strong that you do not possess the inner strength and can call upon an outer power to enable you to overcome it. The burden is never heavier than can be borne. If you strive to live in harmony with the natural laws you will find an inner peace, tranquillity and resolve which will ensure that you always come through.

* * *

To a healer who survived the horrors of a concentration camp, the guide said: It is not possible while you are in your world to have the answers to all the questions that arise in your minds. It is impossible for you to have the fullness of knowledge because you are circumstanced in a world of three dimensions, and occasionally the problems that beset you can be appreciated only when you are able to manifest outside these limited dimensions.

These problems involve considerations of a spiritual nature that you cannot solve, because perforce you can look at them only from the viewpoint of earthly life. You cannot measure them in relationship to the infinity of living which is compulsory for every human being.

So this is where the element of faith arises.

You begin by adding knowledge to faith. Then you arrive at the stage when you must add faith to knowledge. You are in the realm of what is speculation, because you cannot get the answers that would appeal to your reason.

When I say faith, I do not mean credulous, irrational faith. I mean the faith that is founded on knowledge, a faith founded on that sure base of incontrovertible evidence that cannot be gainsaid, and leaves you in no doubt about the spiritual realities which are the basis of all being.

I cannot promise even those I love that they will be exempt from problems. By the very nature of earthly life you must endure these problems. You must grapple with them. You must call on latent, divine power within yourself to help you. If that is insufficient, go one step higher and call on the greater wisdom that streams from the infinite storehouse.

If you have had no problems, you would be akin to spineless automatons, puppets, marionettes. You have infinite possibilities that have to be developed to their fullest extent whilst you are on earth.

The only way this can happen is not when the sun is shining, not if you are living in a bed of roses, not when all is quiet and peaceful and tranquil, but when the storm is raging. It is then that the challenge calls forth this latent power, and you develop. You unfold the spiritual nature within.

In reality your troubles are your greatest friends. They are the means by which you find yourself. Therefore, paradoxically though it may seem, you must welcome troubles when they arise, and realise that in reality they wear the mask of friendship for you.

I always say, "Look back when crisis comes, and see how the signposts of the spirit have always pointed the way, even in the darkest hours when it seemed that no answer could be forthcoming." Look back in your own life, the tragedies that embroiled you, the situations that seemed impossible of relief or even escape, the difficulties that posed their greatest challenges.

Even in the worst of your earthly experiences you were led unfailingly to where you are today, and that guidance will never desert you.

There is a pattern in all human life, and it repeats itself. Especially is this the case in the lives of those who have a service to render. There are no chances, no coincidences, no miracles. The supreme fact about the whole of life in its infinite variations is that the law runs throughout the vast universe, and nothing and nobody is outside the operation of natural law.

15: Mediumship – The Path To Knowledge

Mediumship, in its various forms, is essential to the Other-Side plan.

Without mediums, no contact between Earth and the spirit world would be possible. No teachings could be imparted; no proof of survival beyond death could be garnered.

★   ★   ★

Mediums demonstrate that man is a spiritual being with a spiritual destiny.

It is always a great pleasure and privilege for me to meet any of our co-operators with us in spreading divine truths which are so much needed in your sick, violent, destructive world of today. The opportunities for service are there for all who are ready to help.

Even you are not always aware of the tremendous help that you have received at times when you needed it most.

Death cannot separate those whom love and affection have joined. You demonstrate it so many times to others, so you must know it is a truth which will always be yours. If you do not always succeed in winning the esteem and co-operation of those who should be your closest allies, you must be sorry for them because they have had the opportunities and have not taken them.

The work will not fail. The power of the spirit will not be dissipated. The breakthrough that has been established will never cease. The bridgeheads have been consolidated. They will continue to extend and increase as opportunities and conditions make this possible.

"We seem to have so many barriers to overcome, and difficulties and opposition to face."

These are good for you. You have to face the challenges, the obstacles, difficulties, frustrations and irritations often caused by those who should not create them. But this is the problem on which we constantly engage ourselves.

You know the phrase, "How the angels weep." We weep because we do our best. Then we see that the one who should be serving turns away from the path and the glorious opportunity is lost. But the work will go on.

"What does worry me is that in the past we had many wonderful and dedicated people to do the work. It seems to be more necessary now, yet it is difficult to find the right people."

It is because they have not had enough of the challenges to face and hurdles to overcome. That is why you should welcome all these. When you come to my world you will thank the Great Spirit for all those difficulties and take for granted the things that were easy. The easy ones are no problem.

"We have lost the mediums. Spiritualism is built on mediumship. We wonder what is going to happen as far as new mediums are concerned."

You must try to realise there is an overall plan

conceived by the highest intelligences in our world. I have been present at some of their council meetings. This plan has taken cognisance of every possible factor. The blueprint is there, and it will fulfil itself in your world.

The Great Spirit, filled with infinite wisdom, created man with a measure of relative free will. He could make a choice as to whether he would be a selfish individual concerned only with his own material desires and welfare.

That is the choice, but advisedly I use the words "relative free will." This allows man to hamper, delay, obstruct temporarily what I call the infinite processes of creation. But man cannot halt them. He cannot prevent the divine plan from fulfilling itself in your world.

You talk about the lack of mediums. There are sufficient mediums for the services that are to be performed at this stage of your evolution. As people are ready to receive, so more mediums will be provided.

They will not necessarily come within the purview of any organisation. They may be in home circles, or individuals working on their own. They may not even call themselves Spiritualists, mediums, psychics or even sensitives. But the label does not matter; the service is important.

No call for help, no desire to serve will go unheeded as far as we are concerned. We know your spiritual, mental and physical requirements. We will supply all that is needed at the time when you need it. But we can do things only in our way and in our time; we cannot do them in your way and in your time.

Forgive me if I say that you are not the best judges of

when the time is appropriate for spirit power to descend. All is determined by the state of the soul. If it is ready to receive, it will do so. If it is not ready to receive, there is nothing we can do.

It is true there is to some extent a lack of spiritual education. It is also true unfortunately that we see vanity, egotism and guide worship. Fundamentals are neglected while bypaths are explored that have no real contribution to make to your world.

If you could be where I am, you would banish every possible shadow of worry, fear or apprehension as to what the morrow will bring. You have the greatest power in the universe working through you. It will not fail.

"I suppose we do have to make decisions."

That is your element of free will. Do the best you can is all we expect of you. If you were perfect, you would not be in your world. You have the inestimable privilege of serving others. That is the most important contribution you can make. That is why you were born into your world.

Every soul in your world gets the opportunity to fulfil itself. The natural laws are so devised that none can be outside their operation. They are inexorable and never fail. The seasons automatically follow one another. The tide ebbs and flows with ceaseless mathematical regularity. The flowers, trees, birds, the whole of creation always sings its paean of praise to the supreme power that devised such a wondrous plan on earth in which everything fulfils itself according to its nature.

We will never neglect you; we will not withdraw.

The power of the spirit has come to stay. None can banish it, and it will fulfil its divine purpose.

Throughout all the centuries there have been sporadic upsurges which have failed for a variety of reasons. It will not happen again.

Your world is at a precarious stage of its evolution. It is almost seemingly a touch-and-go situation. You will come through. Pay no heed to the Cassandras, to the prophets and criers of woe.

The Great Spirit has placed a limit on the damage and harm that can be done by man in your world. There is no power in your world that is able to destroy the whole of it. There is no power that can kill the physical bodies of all who dwell in it. There is a limit to what man can do with the most complicated, efficient technological devices that he can invent.

The power of the spirit is stronger than any power of matter that can be produced. Matter is inferior to spirit. Spirit is king and matter is servant. Spirit is supreme, matter exists only because of spirit operating through it. When spirit withdraws, matter disintegrates. Spirit is the overruling power to ensure that you will come through.

Base your confidence on the knowledge which should be the foundation of all your philosophy. When you are confronted with situations where your present knowledge cannot help you, then add some faith to it, founded on what you know. Faith has its part to play when it is reasoned, logical and credible.

Trust us, and we will help you whenever the time is ripe. When the conditions are necessary and right we can produce physical results in your world. We have done it many times, and we will continue. Tell your people we will not fail them. Let them make sure they will not fail us.

If money is lacking it will be found. No worthwhile cause is ever lost because the means have not been there. Is that not true? Have you not found the money is available when required? No servant of the spirit will lack the necessities of physical living. We will provide them. They will not go hungry. They will not starve, they will come through.

Do you know the words *"sursum corda"*? They mean, "keep up your heart." So much has been shown to you, the sublimity of the power of the spirit, the most majestic force in the universe, the most radiant, the most beautiful, glorious and effective. It cannot fail. Do the best you can. That is all we ask of you. And do not be pessimistic.

You have seen the light of the sun. When the clouds obscure it, remember they are only clouds that will gradually fade away and allow the radiance of the sun to illumine once again. The sun is still shining even when you cannot see it.

★ ★ ★

It was characteristic of Silver Birch to give a specially warm welcome to a medium paying his first visit to the circle.

If I can be of any service to you, then I am fulfilling myself, as you fulfil yourself by utilising the gifts of the spirit which have been bestowed on you.

"I am very fortunate," she replied.

Yes, we are all very fortunate because we are the possessors of knowledge which has enriched our beings.

I am always very happy to meet instruments of the spirit because I know the difficulties under which they labour, the challenges they have to meet. I know the story of their pilgrimage from doubt, difficulty and despair to knowledge, certainty and enlightenment.

A similar pattern is revealed in all their earthly lives. There is the time of seeming crucifixion when life has dealt its hardest blow. There have been crises when all foundations seem to have disappeared, sorrow has entered into the mind, the heart is troubled. They feel there is nowhere to turn for guidance and under-standing.

It has to be that those who are to render service must pass through the crucible of suffering. They have to be tried and tested almost to the seeming limits of endur-ance. They have to descend to the depths when no one in their world is capable apparently of lending a sup-porting hand.

It is then that the soul is touched and ready to receive all the richness, power, guidance, wisdom and love that we have to offer. The object of these hard experiences is to produce compassion, for without it no medium or healer is capable of helping those they would serve.

But the way must be like that. How else could the spirit come into its own — in ease, when the sun is shining, when there are no problems? How else can its sublimity be revealed except in the hour of trial and testing? If you never learned anything, what state of mental development would you reach?

There will come a time when you look back and say, "I thank the Great Spirit for all the troubles because they enabled me to have a true understanding of life's purpose and showed the way to fulfil myself."

Always compensation is provided and the balance is inevitably struck. The Great Spirit, being infallible, makes no mistakes. You, like all who serve, can look back and see how the signposts of the spirit have unerringly pointed the way.

You are privileged to be a channel for the greatest power in the world. It flows through you; it inspires you; it enables you to help people who believe they are helpless, just as you once did. You can perform for them a tremendous act of service which cannot be done by clergymen, scientists and philosophers because, alas, the power of the spirit cannot operate through them.

If you help only one soul to find itself, if you comfort only one mourner, if you heal only one sick person, then the whole of your earthly life is justified. How privileged you are to be aware of the tremendous power that is around and about you, that enfolds you, guards you, directs you and ensures that you will continue to unfold your latent divinity and the gifts which are your cherished possession.

"To be good mediums, must one suffer? I have known mediums to suffer all through their lives. I have always been a Spiritualist; I never wanted to be a medium until I lost my child."

It is only in darkness that you can find the light. The whole of life is a polarity. Without suffering your soul would not be ready. Suffering is the catalyst. It is the means by which you emerge better in spirit, more equipped, ready to serve.

"Would you say a medium has to be born, and otherwise cannot be trained?"

You must have the gift; it is bestowed on you. Potentially all are mediums in the sense that, being spiritual beings, they have the attributes of the spirit.

"So many people live their whole lives and are never touched by the spirit because they are materialists."

You should feel sorry for them because they have wasted their earthly lives. They have not fulfilled themselves. They are like children who have gone to school for the requisite time, learnt none of its lessons and thus are not equipped for the adult life that follows when the school period is over.

Earth is an essential preparation for the existence that inevitably follows when death comes. Every happening is part of the price to be paid for evolution. Earthly life cannot be a monotone. It must have its light and shade, its sunshine and storm.

The extremes and the opposites enable you to appreciate what life truly has to offer. There is a saying in your world that action and reaction are equal and opposite. Those who hate can use the same power to change it into love. Hate and love are two sides of the same coin; the choice is yours.

The natural law is perfect in its operation. Just as there is compensation, there is retribution. No one can cheat the laws of the Great Spirit. You can pretend to yourself and to others. Death strips away the mask of pretence and presents the soul as it really is, with no disguise being possible. Those who have the clairvoyant eye can see the reality behind the mask that too many people wear.

But you are helping people, you are pointing the way for them. You show them what can be achieved. After that, the responsibility is theirs as to how they utilise this knowledge in their daily lives. So lift your head high always; do not allow yourself to be downcast. There is much work to be done. There are still, alas, millions who are unaware of spiritual realities. We must do what we can to serve them.

You have the inestimable privilege of giving a service that nobody else, not being similarly gifted, can render in your world. Your heart should rejoice to overflowing at the wonderful opportunities presented to you almost daily.

But remember that knowledge always brings responsibility. Never forget that you are entrusted not only with a sublime truth, but with a sublime power, a divine power, the power of life itself, with all that it possesses.

To help to regenerate and vitalise is a great responsibility. You will not be led astray, you will always be shown the way. Go forth. Each day brings you wonderful opportunities to serve that should enable you to have an exhilaration of spirit.

We are all engaged on a mighty task. There is so much to do in your world. What we have achieved is small compared with what is to be achieved. We must press on and always help where we can. We must play our parts in demonstrating that the power of the spirit can truly enrich lives if only people will make themselves accessible to it and derive as a result all that it has to offer.

Your work is blessed because you serve. Pray for greater strength, greater power and greater wisdom so that you can add to your store. Know that even if we who co-operate with you cannot always be seen, heard or felt, we continue to guard, guide, uphold and sustain you.

Thus together we can fulfil the divine plan which is intended to point the way for all the children of the Great Spirit. And as we perform this service, we become more in tune with the overruling power of the Great Spirit.

★ ★ ★

The guide encouraged another medium in these words:

The picture that has been painted of me is somewhat exaggerated insofar as I am not the possessor of all wisdom, truth and power, I am a human being like you are. But I have lived longer than you have, and travelled further on the path of spiritual progress.

As a result I have been able to assimilate more knowledge, which I have found most enlightening in helping to solve many of the problems that perplex people. So I have retraced my footsteps and would like to share whatever I have gained with those who are ready to receive it.

You are very fortunate in the sense that these truths do not come to you like Paul on the road to Damascus, as a blinding flash of light, but as reasonably intelligent and in no way an insult to your mind. You have acquired a knowledge which gives you a better perspective of life, the purpose of incarnating into your world, and what it is you have to achieve so that you fit yourself for the much greater and richer life that starts once you have left your physical body behind, never to inhabit it again.

This knowledge came to you at a time when you were ready to receive it. There had been crises and problems to be resolved. You were searching for the answers which seemingly had not been found in your world.

The soul has to be touched. It slumbers, it is dormant; and the little spark of divinity has to be fanned before it can achieve its brilliant illumination. The catalyst is what you call difficulty, crisis, sorrow, bereavement, ill-health.

Life is a polarity. You must have the opposites of the spectrum, two sides of the coin, what you call good and what you consider bad. But all experiences have their parts to play in helping the soul to find itself. It does not do so in a bed of roses, but only when it is touched by the catalyst that is essential for this purpose. You have the healing gift in embryo, and it can be developed so that you can help others. You have work to do, and the way is being opened for you to do it. You may think that you have finished all that you should do, but you are at the beginning of a new cycle that will open out and bring you much mental and spiritual reward.

For you the future is one of great promise. It will bring adventures of the mind and spirit that will be of a tremendous help to you and to others. Do you know that you and your wife were brought together for this purpose? You must try to realise that you are being guided and impressed. You have noticed how the doors have opened, the way has been shown.

I always tell my friends here that we can only do things in our way and in our time. We wait patiently for you to awaken. It takes many years. Then when you start to become receptive many of you are in a hurry and say, "Let us get on with it."

You forget that we have waited until the time was ripe. We have to exert our influence in your world, which is material, from our world, which is spiritual. We have to use channels, mediums, to do so. If no mediums are available then we have to do it by impression, guidance, influence, and then watch carefully to ensure that you do not even unconsciously block the very channel by which help can come. This is a great problem.

The channel is open and your reception is good when there are complete trust, confidence and faith that are founded on knowledge. The moment fear asserts itself you disturb the atmosphere, you introduce an element that closes the channel. Fear is the child of ignorance. Fear should not make itself felt among those who have knowledge.

Similarly, any thoughts of anxiety act as a deterrent to what can be achieved. Always when I speak through my instrument here the first words I say are, "Let us try to abolish any thoughts of fear, anxiety, worry or apprehension." These are impediments to the full, free flowing of the power of the spirit.

Rest your confidence in us. We will show you the way. We will open the doors. If you knock on a door that is closed and will not open, forget it. The moment you knock on a door and it opens, then you go right through because that is the right entrance for you. There is no other way that we can work. We will help, counsel and lead.

Do not be in a hurry. Just give us willing co-operation and we will fulfil our part.

The guide assured a clairaudient:

You will not be forgotten. The power of the spirit will ensure that you will be sustained in the days that are in front of you, just as you were protected, guarded and guided in the past when you knew not where to turn, when it seemed as if you had reached the abyss of despair.

Continue to express the gifts that the Great Spirit with infinite wisdom has bestowed on you. Serve in places where the power of the spirit has not manifested before, and thus increase the illumination it brings to those who are ready to receive it.

You cannot measure what is being achieved as lives are changed. Because of you, the knowledge comes as a revelation to them. Do not allow yourself to be downcast or have even a shadow of fear as to what the morrow will bring. You have been brought through many crises. The way will be shown to you whenever it is necessary.

You are a channel for the power of the spirit and should be proud of what has been achieved, and prouder still when you realise what is still to be achieved with your co-operation.

You have to earn your bread and butter. You have to provide for the requirements of the physical world. You have to have a roof over your head. You have to wear clothes, and pay for all the other necessities because it is a material world in which you live.

I am aware of all that, but these should not cause anxiety. Responsibility, yes; anxiety, no!

I am very familiar with your world and its workings.

Occasionally I have had to see that certain physical laws are operated to make sure that certain physical results would ensue.

What I always try to stress, to those who are prepared to listen, is that the material is only the reflection, the shadow, the husk, not the reality. The material exists because it is animated by the spirit. If the spirit is right, if there is harmony between spirit, mind and matter, then all that is necessary to sustain you physically will be forthcoming.

Spirit is master, matter is servant. Spirit is king, matter is commoner. Spirit is superior, matter is inferior. It would be foolish for anyone to say that you should ignore the physical requirements which are necessary to maintain you in your world. But it is equally foolish to give them undue attention and to neglect the requirements of your mind and spirit.

This is the great lesson that millions have still to learn in your world. They give priority to matter and very little attention to spirit.

Those who have knowledge of spirit realities should never allow anxiety, fear or worry to effect a lodgment within their beings.

These are negative qualities. These block the channels by which vivifying power can reach you. These are obstructions that bar and interfere with the harmonious conditions which alone can promote what is essential for the fullness of living.

It is always good to be reminded of eternal values, and to instruct those who are prepared to be instructed how to strike the right balance, so that they derive from their lives the richness in all aspects of being that should be theirs.

I look around your world and see millions who are spiritually impoverished. You can have sadness for physical poverty, but it is equally sad to see needless spiritual poverty.

If people would only open their hearts and minds they could be filled with the glory, radiance, dignity, grandeur and nobility that the spirit has to offer. This is part of our mission, to try to get you always to realise what are the rightful priorities in the way that you conduct your lives.

You are richly blessed because the Great Spirit with infinite wisdom conferred on you some of the gifts of the spirit. As a result you have been able to accomplish far more than any bishop or clergyman. You have been able to dry the tears of mourners, give strength to those who were weak mentally and spiritually, to heal the sick, and to direct those who had lost their way. These, like yourself at one time, were at a stage where they thought no help was forthcoming from anybody or anything in your world or in ours.

It is not possible to have divine gifts bestowed on you without the accompanying problem that in order to be able to help others you have to tread a path of affliction and sorrow. You have to suffer because that enables you to fulfil yourself as an instrument of the spirit. The essential experience of suffering is the touchstone for all mediums; then they are truly able to help those who are brought to them.

If you are a servant of the spirit, you must not expect a life of ease.

All those who have work to do and are treading the

spiritual path must find it is not an easy one to follow. If spiritual mastery could be easily attained it would not be worth the having. The prizes of the spirit have to be earned by arduous labour, but once gained they cannot be lost.

The wealth of the spirit is eternal. The wealth you acquire on earth can only have a temporary possession for you.

Spiritual mastery is not easily attained. Neither are the prizes of the spirit speedily gained.

You were born to serve; you have served and you are serving. I am always happy to talk to any of those who are channels for that wondrous, divine power. It is the power of life that brings in its train such a rich beneficence for those who are ready. If they are not ready to receive, there is nothing you can do to help them.

The mere fact of their having been brought to you means they have had the great chance of self-realisation. If it is accomplished, then you should sing for joy. If it is not, then shed a silent tear for the missed opportunity.

You have still work to do. You are fulfilling yourself. You should be full of happiness at the fact that you are able to perform a divine service.

★ ★ ★

Unfortunately there are millions in your world who are completely unaware of the spiritual realities which make it possible for them to live. They have no idea of the purpose of their being, what it is they must do to fulfil themselves and to utilise any talents or gifts, so that they in turn can help others to fulfil themselves.

Every time you are the means by which a soul is touched and begins to come into its own very slowly, you are rendering a service that is very important.

This is why we have made the supreme effort to come back to your world. Populations have lost their way and flounder in a morass of materialistic selfishness, greed and cupidity which bring in their train war, violence and hatred.

Until the supremacy of the spirit is recognised, and people become aware that they are spirits with bodies, that they are endowed with a portion of divinity which links them together in a vast spiritual brotherhood and sisterhood, making them one great family with the Great Spirit as eternal father and mother of them all – only then will you end the wars, violence and hatred.

In their place will reign love, compassion, mercy, tolerance, co-operation, harmony and peace, not only among the humans, but among the animals who share this planet with them. So in time there will be abolished the cruelties that are the dark stains in your world.

This is the whole purpose behind everything we are trying to do. There is no need to be downcast or pessimistic. You should all be optimistic, filled with hope based on faith; not blind, credulous, unreasoning faith, but faith founded on the knowledge you have received and which has given you the incontrovertible evidence that life has a spiritual permanent reality.

"One Positive Thinking teacher says you can have anything, material or spiritual, if you believe it strongly enough. Is this a misuse of psychic power?"

I think the statement would have to be qualified because you cannot have anything that you want. There is a limit imposed by natural law on what you can attain. Were there not this limitation, then man could destroy and oppose the whole principle on which his world and the universe are founded. I am not opposing the idea behind positive thinking, but it would be absurd to say you can have anything you want. Suppose you desire to have the sun, you could not get it.

★   ★   ★

A developing medium sought the guide's advice:
"I have found a difficulty in preparing myself during the daytime so as to be natural when I demonstrate my gift. Because I have just begun, I have much to overcome. Perhaps it will work out in time."

Be as natural as you possibly can. Be natural, be receptive, do not worry, have no fear, be confident. The power that has guided you to where you are now will not fail. The arms of love that hold you in their embrace will not unfold and desert you.

Play your part; we will play ours. In preparation try and achieve a period of quietness. Withdraw to where you are in a condition freed from the strident clangour of your material world and you can allow the inner, divine power to manifest in larger measure and enfold you to provide a calmness, attunement and receptivity which are all you need to perform the service that you render.

Do not be in a hurry; take your time. It took a long time for you to get where you are. You will find that there is a master plan in which we all fit and have our parts to play. It will work itself out not only for you but for us.

★   ★   ★

In the Spiritualist movement's early days, physical

phenomena were widespread.

Levitation of people, the apportation of fresh flowers and other objects, materialisation of human forms that often built before sitters' eyes, and other phenomena that duplicated Bible "miracles" were witnessed by thousands. Now these phenomena are rare.

"Why are physical phenomena so hard to attain?"

Because there is a law not only of physical evolution but of spiritual evolution. The climate of opinion has changed in your world. The physical phenomena were necessary at a time when spiritual realities had to be materially demonstrated. Scientists were not prepared to accept anything that did not come within this category.

Now your world has seen the havoc wrought and the benefits that can be obtained by nuclear fission. The basis of materialism has been split altogether; the indissoluble atom has been dissolved. Scientists accept that matter is not solid, and that reality is to be found in the invisible.

Concurrent with that change in the climate of opinion you have the development and promotion of spiritual healing which, when it succeeds, demonstrates the existence of a power that is superior to matter.

"We hear about experiments that scientists are conducting with regard to psychic phenomena, particularly in the Iron Curtain countries. It would seem that some will be used for purposes that are not constructive."

I am not worried. I have lived longer than any of you. Because of what I have seen, heard and understood I have a great reverence, awe and wonder for the Great Spirit who, with infinite wisdom and love, devised the cosmic scheme that embraces all universes and worlds.

Everybody and everything are regulated by natural laws that are unfailing, always exact in their operation, and never making a mistake.

Nothing and nobody in your world can be excluded, forgotten or neglected because the natural laws encompass them all. From the most majestic to the most minute, from the simple to the complex, natural law governs, sustains and regulates every phase of being.

If man were not greedy and lived in harmony with the natural laws, nature would be profligate with the abundance it has to offer.

The natural laws impose limitations for people in your world. They cannot do anything contrary to the natural laws. There are restrictions fixed by the natural laws on the amount of damage and destruction that the people of your world can do.

So I am an optimist and not a pessimist. The experiments to which you refer are designed primarily because it is thought they have some military value. Whatever damage they can do is comparatively small to the good that can be done by those who use science and technology, and all the massive power available, to bring benefits to the world in which you live.

Do not fear. Fear is a bad counsellor. Fear corrodes; fear rusts; fear blocks the channels through which help can come. The Great Spirit is in charge of your world and all worlds, and goodness will triumph over evil.

"You wouldn't deny that psychic gifts can be used for evil and improper purposes."

The Great Spirit created you, not as puppets or marionettes. You were given a measure of free will, a choice. But it is restricted and limited. You cannot behave contrary to the natural laws.

If you have psychic gifts you can abuse them. That is your responsibility. You cannot have knowledge without the responsibility to which that knowledge is put.

16: The Enigma of Religion

Though teachers have brought spiritual enlightenment throughout the ages, man in his ignorance has misunderstood much.

All religions have a grain of truth; but when man makes bread to feed the multitude, often he throws away the wheatgerm with the chaff.

Silver Birch's first comments will surprise many.

★ ★ ★

"People I have met state they are confirmed Spiritualists, yet they follow their orthodox religions. Should not they put behind these ideas when they accept Spiritualism?"

I am not bothered with these labels. I am not sure whether I am a Spiritualist, because I have not been confirmed. What you call yourself does not matter. We are concerned with the way you live your life.

Religion, what is it? Is it going to church, synagogue, chapel or temple? Is it the acceptance of certain theological ideas devised by man? Is it calling yourself a Roman Catholic, a Protestant, a Buddhist, a Jew?

Religion is living in a way that brings you closer to the Great Spirit. Religion is when the Great Spirit is expressed in your actions. Religion is service.

If you find there are some people who have all the

161

benefits of communication with our world but still adhere to certain conventional theological beliefs, then be sorry for them. Say a silent prayer for them because they are still only on the first rungs of the ladder, or are in the half-way stage.

Recognise that it is not always easy to abandon the teaching received in childhood, when the mind was plastic and impressionable and accepted without question what was given to it. Gradually these theological ideas become part of the warp and weft of the subconscious mind, are embedded in its depths, and an individual finds it almost impossible to rid himself of them.

Be patient. There was a time when all of us had ideas which we believed, but later wisdom made us abandon them. After all, none of us has attained the summit of perfection; to do so will require eternity. Be tolerant. Help them. Do not argue with them; that gets nowhere. In such discussion, as the poet said, they leave by the same door by which they came in.

Be patient with those who cannot see further than their theological noses. Time will work its will with them, as it has with you.

★ ★ ★

"Many people are very depressed for no reason. What has come over the young people? Are they spiritually starved?"

They have not found their way. They have come into a world where violence rules. They believe their elders have betrayed them. They feel also that they can obtain no guidance from conventional religion.

"Do you think too much blame has been put on the elders?

Everyone has his own path to find."

I am not agreeing with their outlook. I am only explaining it, because in time they will become elders.

"There is no substitute for experience."

Your bad experiences are the best for you. Your good experiences are often the worst for you. My friends have heard me say many times that the virtue of falling down is that you can pick yourself up.

* * *

A visitor asked about the world's creation, citing the description in Genesis. In some quarters it was believed that creatures from outer space came to earth for this purpose, he said.

Of course you are now addressing your question to an out-of-space creature! Do not be bothered by what it says in Genesis or in any other book. If it is unacceptable to your reason, dismiss it. How did your world begin is what you want to know.

"There are many theories; we really don't know."

Let me say that I have a little more than a theory. I have a little knowledge on this subject. Your world has always existed. It had no beginning, nor will it have an end. If you want to quote from the Bible, you have statements like the one attributed to the Nazarene, "Before Abraham was I am."

Spirit has always existed: it was not spontaneously created. It slumbered for millions of years until the rudimental beginnings of life gradually manifested in your world. Life is spirit and spirit is life. It always has had the potentials of infinity.

There were no creatures from outer space to create the beginnings of life in your world. Life was always there, and developed, unfolded and progressed according to the natural laws of evolution that infinite intelligence devised.

"I understand that now a good deal of Darwin's theory is being disputed, though at the time he was accepted. There seem to be facts which he missed."

There are always facts that are missed because all knowledge is not available at any stage of evolution. Only perfection contains all knowledge, and perfection has not yet been attained in your world or in mine. Let me say categorically that evolution, physical, mental and spiritual, is part of the operation of natural law.

"I am not very keen on the thought of being descended from monkeys."

It may also be true that monkeys are not very keen on the idea! In the sight of the Great Spirit monkeys are as precious as humans.

★   ★   ★

Silver Birch has always expressed great love for Jesus, whom he calls "The Nazarene."

It has been my privilege many times with colleagues in my world to be present at conferences, congresses, meetings, call them whatever you like. At these the Nazarene refers to many of the plans the hierarchy devised to ensure that the power of the spirit should remain in your world.

The Nazarene is one of the hierarchy behind all the directives we receive when we leave your world occasionally to fortify ourselves to cope with our missions and to glean more of what it is we have to achieve.

I have a great reverence for Jesus, the Nazarene, a wondrous example of what the power of the spirit could achieve when divinity assumes human form and gives to those available simple but profound teaching that love is a power that solves all problems when people allow themselves to be animated by it.

The Nazarene demonstrated the same spiritual phenomena that we make available today, because their operation is due to the same natural laws which always have been, which still are in existence, and will continue to be so.

Having attracted the multitudes by what were wrongly called miracles, he taught the great truths of the spirit: love thy neighbour as thyself, do good to those who hurt you; the essence of all religions.

But the difference is this, that with his passing into our world the mission of Jesus did not end. He is still at work, inspiring those who continue to see and meet him, to propound these truths, to demonstrate these phenomena so that those who are ready would play their part in helping the infinite, creative power of the Great Spirit to flow through an increasing number of channels everywhere.

We have nothing but respect and reverence for Jesus. But we do not have that respect and reverence for many of his followers who have worshipped and continue to worship Jesus, yet pay no heed to his teachings. Instead of the truth he taught unifying them, it divides them.

In your world today there are black areas where the same followers of the Nazarene persecute and kill one another. They do not understand his mission. If you believe in the Nazarene and realise that love is the greatest power in the universe, you should not kill or commit acts of violence against others who say they believe in those same principles.

"It must be very agonising to the Nazarene to see, as indeed do so many of you in the spirit world, what has been done in his name on earth."

Yes, and he has shed many tears. After all, he is not responsible for what others do. You who call yourselves Spiritualists proclaim one of our greatest principles, that every individual is personally responsible for his or her acts.

"What did Jesus look like?"

The Nazarene has been described many times by people in our world. He is not as painted by artists living in varying countries and according to their cultures. He is very much like the kind of people among whom he moved during his ministry. Were he different, then he would not have fulfilled his mission.

"Some mediums speak of a Cosmic Christ. Others see Christ as an individual spirit. Are they two different aspects for the same existence?"

You are allowing names to bother you. There is the man Jesus, whose surname was not Christ, and there is what is called the Christ power, the power of the spirit. If you differentiate between the man and the power that animated him, you have the clearest picture of all.

"Would it be possible by automatic writing or some other means to tell us exactly what Jesus said?"

I don't know. The difficulty is that no one recorded the utterances of the Nazarene at the time and so memory would have to play its part. His main teaching was the gospel of love. "Love thy neighbour as thyself. Do good to those who hurt you." Love is the fulfilling of the law. What else is required to help mankind? Love is the highest expression of the spirit. Love is what the Great Spirit has to offer. Love is what we offer you.

The object of the Nazarene's mission was to demonstrate spiritual reality. If the Nazarene were to reappear in your world today and to repeat what he said 2,000 years ago I doubt if anyone would listen.

"You said so many people arrive in the spirit world with false teaching. In St John's gospel it says believing is the important part."

No. Everyone will live after what you call death, not because of believing in a creed, a doctrine or dogma, but because it is an unalterable natural law. It has nothing to do with religion. It is a law as equal to the law of cause and effect.

What you have quoted is one of the interpolations in the Bible which has caused great affliction and separated people. Is it not paradoxical that a book, a religious book, a holy book, a sacred book, has caused more bloodshed than an ordinary volume could have done? Yet the purpose of religion should be to unite everybody in a common brotherhood and sisterhood because of their unbreakable fundamental spiritual relationship.

"Was the body of Jesus crucified?"

Do you want my opinion? It does not matter. What matters is what Jesus taught. You will go on arguing for ever about what happened at the crucifixion.

I cannot prove what I say about that, and so I will not attempt to answer your question. I do not like to condemn others. That is not my mission.

My mission is to draw attention to the spiritual principles on which life is founded. It seems to me that you worry a great deal about things which do not matter. Whether the Nazarene was crucified or not will make no difference to the evolution of your soul.

Concentrate on the vital matters in life. Here you are in a world with opportunities to play your part, to help others, to develop your spiritual nature and to fulfil yourselves. Don't worry overmuch about whether there are people on Mars, whether you will resurrect in a thousand years.

What matters is how you comport yourselves in your daily lives. Do the best you can. By doing so, you will enjoy a greater harmony with the Great Spirit. And as a result you will feel that radiance, tranquillity, repose and confidence that come to all those who seek to make the will of the Great Spirit their will.

17: Violence – The Way of Self-pity

Mankind's history is dark with greed, aggression and oppression. Bitterness still festers and erupts in many parts of the globe, siring fear in millions who wish to live in peace.

Silver Birch offers these words to the despairing.

★ ★ ★

Your world is in a ferment. It is partly due to the upheavals caused by two world wars. In a ferment sometimes not always the best comes to the top.

What you are really seeing take place is the dim outline of a new world. Birth is not always a beautiful or painless process.

Violence is a form of mass-emotion, a kind of hysteria born of inferiority, a self-pity that desires to draw attention to itself as the only means of making others aware of their existence.

It is not an easy life that you live in your world today; it is a very difficult one. You have violence on an ever-increasing scale. You have greed, selfishness, rapacity and all the other cancerous happenings that are a sore on the world body.

Millions have lost their way; millions worship false gods; millions have no idea of what life is all about, and what they have to do to fulfil themselves. It is not only true of your country, but of many lands which are far worse than the one in which you dwell. Greed and avarice, by-products of materialism, have taken command of people who worship this false god. They all desire the golden calf which they regard as the acme of all attainment.

They have no understanding of eternal verities. Their allegiance is to materialism, the festering cancer of your world, but it does not affect the whole of its inhabitants.

Do not let it trouble you unduly. There is nothing you can do about it, except to show an example in your own lives of how those who are the ambassadors of the spirit should comport themselves. You will not be harmed, but protected as in the days that have gone. I have said it before, "Lift up your hearts."

Let others be fearful, and despair of what the morrow will bring. You have nothing to fear. No problem, no obstacle, no handicap will come your way that you will not be able to overcome. Call on the divine power within and the even greater divine power without, to which you have access.

It is difficult in the turmoil and turbulence, the strife, anxiety and trouble of your world to remember that these affect only the physical.

Your soul cannot be damaged. Your body may be, but the soul will always be ready to perform its task.

"Will man ever live a life of peace with his fellows instead of warring?"

That is very difficult to answer. What you must appreciate is that the Great Spirit endowed man with an element of free will. Human beings could have been created as puppets. That free will provides man with the opportunity of helping what I call the infinite processes of creation.

Man has the chance to make the world in which he lives a garden of Eden, a paradise, a heaven, just as he can make it a dark, desolate and grim forbidding world. That is the measure of his choice.

You have war, violence, greed, cupidity, selfishness, because materialism predominates.

Materialism exists because the vast majority of people in your world do not realise there is a life beyond physical death, despite the teaching of the many religions.

Millions do not accept the fact of an inevitable afterlife which is really tangible, where there is compensation and retribution. They believe that earth is the only life they will ever have. So logically they argue that if the physical is all, let us have the best it has to offer. This is the cause of war. This leads people to hate, to subjugate, to imprison and even to kill one another.

That is not the whole of the picture. I have paid tribute to the infallibility of the natural law which also places a restriction on the havoc that man can wreak in your world.

We are engaged in the mighty task of helping to bring an understanding of spiritual realities wherever we can.

Mediums demonstrate that man is a spiritual being with a spiritual destiny. Man makes or mars his destiny according to the way he conducts himself. The law is unfailing in its sequence of cause and effect, of sowing and reaping.

Whatever good you do, you are the better for it. Whatever selfishness you practise, you are the worse for it. You cannot cheat the natural law. You cannot say on your deathbed that you are sorry for what you have done, and automatically obliterate all the effects of the causes you set in motion.

As this truth gradually is accepted by an increasing number of people, so wars will lessen and peace obtain a greater hold in larger areas of your world. That is the only answer I can give. It cannot be done overnight.

Play your part. Do the best you can. Help those who come to you. Be kind, tolerant, compassionate. Serve where the opportunities come. And that is how you will help.

★   ★   ★

"Does the anguish that we sometimes find around come not from without but from within?"

It can be both. What you must appreciate is that earthly life provides a polarity which is not available in our world. In our world people of the same stage of evolution are in the same spiritual sphere or plane.

In your world you are mixing all the time with people of varying stages of evolution. You get opportunities for all the opposites to be encountered. Thus you can have light and dark, heat and cold. All this is the purpose of earthly life. It provides the means by which the soul comes into its own.

It is the school where you learn the lessons which fit you for that larger world which one day you will inhabit. If you have anguish, it is because by so doing you will be able to appreciate joy, its opposite.

There is a saying, which I have often quoted, that things can be equal and opposite, the two sides of the same coin. It is in the variety of experience that the soul finds itself. This is the equivalent to the process of the hardening of the steel, the emergence of the gold after being crushed from its ore.

"I perceive in many people what I believe to be a mental revolution. I believe this is a natural sequence which our spirit friends are organising, and the timing is now."

Your world is in a melting-pot. You are seeing the war between good and evil, similar to the story told in the Bible. You are also seeing the unfortunate results of the worship of mammon, the pursuit of greed and avarice, the desire for material power, the subjection of all that is noble, elevating, spiritual; the selfishness that I call the festering cancer of your world.

At the same time religion, in its conventional sense, has lost its potency, influence and validity to guide and direct. Allegiance to false doctrines that make no sense to those who have intelligence means that an increasing number continue to turn their backs on what the conventional religions have to offer.

In addition science has started on the wrong road, with massive appliances that pose the crucial question mark of whether they will be used to benefit humanity or wreak destruction in your world. That is the crucial time in which you live, and it is the reason why we make a supreme effort.

This is to influence, to guide, to direct and to point the only way by which peace, harmony, amity, concord and co-operation can be achieved.

We are trying to demonstrate that all who live on earth are part of a vast spiritual family, that what you call God, and I the Great Spirit, is the supreme father of them all.

We will win this fight. You and others are part of the vast army of the spirit engaged in this battle. So you all have to be tried and tested to ensure that you will not fail in the great task to which you have been assigned.

Spirit is stronger than matter. There is no power in the world of matter that is greater than the divine power, which will triumph, though it will take time.

There is no room for pessimism or despair among those who have knowledge. The Great Spirit constructed man with the head at the top so that he could look up. Were he intended to look down, his head would be where his feet are.

Every soul engaged in the task of liberating humanity must go through the tests and challenges. They are essential parts of the spiritual development. There is no other way. When you come to our world and look back, you will thank the Great Spirit for all the difficulties, and realise they were most important parts of your earthly life.

Your world has had prophecies of disasters for a long time. Often dates have been given when your world would be destroyed. There is no second coming. The Nazarene accomplished his earthly mission – two thousand years ago. He continues his mission in the larger life which I inhabit. His is the guiding influence that directs our activities.

Your world will not be destroyed overnight. The Great Spirit, with infinite love and wisdom, has devised natural laws which provide for every facet of being, mighty or minute, complex or simple. The natural laws operate by evolution, not revolution. They ensure that the power of man is restricted. There are things he cannot do. He has a measure of free will, but it is limited.

"Do you think that the world, when it comes to the New Age, will have a much increased consciousness compared with what it has had so far?"

To me there is a constant process of evolution, development, unfoldment. It will not happen that overnight there will be a change and a new age will be ushered in. Gradually, as truth progresses, more and more people will become aware of it.

Once they realise that the whole of the universe is founded on spiritual realities that cannot fail, and as a result they begin to live these implications, so there will be higher states of consciousness and awareness functioning in your world, but it will all be a gradual process.

"Will the Age of Aquarius herald any real changes in our world?"

Your world is always changing, not only physically but spiritually. You must accept the fact that, as there is a law of evolution, there must be changes as it occurs. Evolution means the gradual development from one condition to another that is higher than its predecessor.

"Can you tell us something about the future of our world?"

Your world will continue to exist because there is no individual or combinations of individuals who have the power to destroy the whole of it. There is a limitation placed upon the harm that can be done and the means that you can use, or can be invented or discovered, to wreak damage on such a vast scale that the world would cease to be tenable.

Have no fear, the will of the Great Spirit must always

prevail. Be positive, optimistic and constructive in your outlook, and play your part. Banish fear, worry, apprehension, anything that stops the rich power of the spirit from filling you and encouraging you to do the best you can. That is all we ask of you. Do the best you can. No one can do better than his best.

Have no fear of what the morrow will bring. The morrow is the herald of glorious opportunities for you to unfold latent divinity, to enjoy life in all its fullness, physically, mentally and spiritually, becoming increasingly aware of that wondrous spiritual radiance that is always round and about you.

★ ★ ★

"Do you believe capital punishment will solve our problems like violence?"

You will not solve your problems that way at all. Love is the fulfilling of the law. Whatever you do must be an attempt to help, not to exact revenge.

Another murder does not excuse the first one. Killing by the State does not solve any situation. If you meet force by force you are not encouraging the powers of goodness, compassion and kindness to be exercised.

All punishment must be remedial and redemptive. The object should always be to try and enable the soul to come into its own. To send into our world souls that are unready merely increases problems. It does not lessen them in your world or in ours. Besides, you can make mistakes.

"Two points occur to me. Suppose persons were precipitated into the next world swiftly, with all their sins heavy upon them, you might say. It is often argued that in this state

they merely come back and influence other people with like tendencies. *Therefore they do more damage after they had been transported to the next world than if they had been allowed to remain.*

"Why can your side of life not deal with these who are in essence sick souls, take care of them just as we might, and so prevent them influencing others in the same direction?"

It is not easy. Every second there are coming into our world souls not ready for it. We don't want an increase. All our efforts are directed to helping people to live on earth as they should, so that they are ready for life in our world.

The whole object of our coming back to your world is to preach the gospel of love, which the Nazarene taught. You must love and not hate one another, or exact revenge.

A Nigerian chief asked Silver Birch for his assessment of justice.

"I ask because in human conditions we attempt to administer justice. We look at the two sides and say one will be guilty. Is there any divine limit to the human understanding of justice?"

You cannot limit divine justice. Being divine it will operate, just like nature, irrespective of what you wish, think or desire. You cannot make comparisons between divine and human justice. Human justice is fallible, makes mistakes; the innocent is sometimes guilty and the guilty is sometimes innocent. Being human you must err, because you cannot be infallible.

Divine justice is infallible. It cannot make mistakes, because of the law of cause and effect which is unfailing in its operation. You cannot interpose anything between cause and effect; the sequence is unbreakable, inevitable, unalterable. Were it not so, justice would not be divine and the Great Spirit cease to be perfect.

Being human, you will make mistakes. Your judges will give wrong decisions. Your man-made laws cannot apprehend and apply to every condition in your human society. New factors arise for which your laws have not made provision, because they did not foresee them.

The natural laws have foreseen every circumstance, because the Great Spirit is perfect. Nothing is forgotten, nothing is overlooked. All must operate within the framework of natural law. One day perhaps, when wisdom rules your countries, you will choose judges not only for their knowledge of law, but also because their clairvoyance has been sufficiently developed to enable them to see who is innocent and who is guilty.

"Could we say divine justice, which is the natural law, is infallible, but human justice is not infallible? Does that paraphrase what we have been talking about? It is not infallible because we are ordinary, sinful human beings without the full knowledge of the natural law."

I call that a good paraphrase, but I do not like to call you sinful.

"The New Testament says, 'Sin is lawlessness; not in operation'."

We love you because you are human. If you were perfect there would be no point in our coming to you. Probably you would be coming to us to help us on our way.

A detective making his first visit to the circle remarked:

"In my profession I have seen many people destroyed and taken away before their time because of some ferocious act. I have often wondered if it were possible for somebody to talk

to them to ensure that this could not happen again."

Unfortunately too many of them become earth-bound, and it takes a long time for enlightenment to come to free them from this self-created prison. It is a difficult problem on which I could enlarge. The true object of their treatment should not be revenge, which is a wrong emotion, but remedial, an attempt at rehabilitation. Justice is not revenge.

"I thought justice was prevention."

But too often revenge takes priority. In the Old Testament it was "An eye for an eye and a tooth for a tooth." But in the New Testament the Nazarene taught not only loving one's neighbour but even loving those who hate you. The acid test is the motive all the time. If the motive is right, all things will work out.

★   ★   ★

A journalist sought the guide's advice on her work.

"I have been asked to research and write about warnings that have come to mankind from the spirit world and from other worlds. One stated that nuclear power was evil and should stop, and also spoke about the selfishness of mankind. I would like your voice to be heard. If you have any particular warning, could you formulate it, please?"

I do not regard your nuclear power as evil. The use made of it can be evil. On the other hand, the use that can be made of it could be of tremendous benefit to your world. The decision lies with those who are capable of directing or misdirecting this tremendous power.

As to warnings, do not assume for one moment that we have the equivalent spirit Cassandras who are saying, "Woe, woe, woe," because there are dreadful cataclysms coming to you.

The position is not simple. The Great Spirit has given His children a measure of free will within limits, so that they can either fill your world with radiance, beauty, glory and abundance or make it a hell on earth. It is man who has this choice.

The more that technology produces, and reveals tremendous powers which it can unleash, so the responsibility becomes heavier as to how these are to be used in your world. There is no other way, so far as I can understand, that the processes of evolution could be accomplished, except that man, a child of a divine parent, with all the divine potential, should be allowed to express that, and flood your world with all the beauty that it could have, and help nature to release its massive bounty for all to share.

That is the choice for man to have. But if he ignores it and worships the god of mammon, is greedy, selfish, avaricious, and cares not for his neighbour and nobody else but himself, then automatically he will fill his country and the world with all the darkness, difficulty, evils, pestilence and disease which are the fruits of a misused free will.

But having said that, we stress that no matter how much power man has at his disposal, it has no comparison with the infinite power which has set limits on all the destruction and havoc that man can wreak in your world. He cannot destroy the entire world or the universe in which he lives.

"So it is still God's world."

Yes, it is still the Great Spirit's world and the Great

Spirit must prevail. God is infinite, God is divine love and wisdom, and God provides all His children with the means of sharing in a heavenly kingdom on earth if they so desire.

If you were puppets, marionettes, robots, your life would be meaningless and purposeless. There would be no evolution, no gradual growth towards perfection. It would become a kind of eternal limbo of nothingness. That is not the object.

I who have lived much longer than any of you have learned to regard with awe, wonder, respect and admiration the universal framework that divine perfection has created. Nothing can destroy the operation of laws that infinite intelligence devised.

There is no need for those with knowledge, who are privileged to have a glimpse of the eternal principles upon which all life is governed, to have fear for the future. Despite your technological wonders, your scientific achievements, which can be used for good or ill, there is a limit to the havoc that man can wreak in your world. He has not unfettered, unlimited freedom to destroy the whole of your world and the physical bodies of those who dwell in it.

Love is greater than hate. Spirit is superior to matter. The mightiest power in the universe emanates from the Great Spirit of all life. The natural laws, created by infinite intelligence and governed by divine wisdom, will ensure that slowly and inevitably there will come a better world than the one in which you live.

18: Our Lesser Brethren?

Silver Birch has always stressed man's responsibility to every creature.

★ ★ ★

Alas, because of lack of spiritual development, there are millions of people on earth who do not realise that the spirit which animates them is the same one that animates all the creatures who share the planet with them. They do not see them as spirits with earthly bodies, just as they are.

They do not realise that because they believe they are superior to the animals, they have a responsibility towards them, because the higher should always help what it believes is the lower.

You have needless cruelty and terror inflicted on innocent creatures in the false belief that through this vicious means health will be attained by humans. This is not true.

The long-term problem is to spread the knowledge of spiritual realities so that these wicked and often diabolical experiments should altogether cease. You have to reach the stage where man has developed his conscience to know that what he is doing is wrong.

"Why should animals suffer at the hands of humans? Were they put here only to test our spiritual growth? Why were they not put on another physical plane whose inhabitants were

highly-evolved beings who would love and help their spiritual evolution?"

The same question could be asked as to why humans are put into your world to suffer at the hands of other humans. Why cannot they be put elsewhere where they cannot suffer?

What you have to realise is that the whole of earthly life is a preparatory school, a training ground where man is given the opportunity to manifest in the largest possible manner the divinity within him.

He has, to a limited degree, the free will to decide his actions. As a result he advances or holds back the progress that he has to achieve in your world or in mine, so that the spirit evolves and gradually sheds the imperfections on its eternal path of progress.

When you have free will then it is patent that some will exercise it wrongfully, vengefully, ignorantly, and others will suffer as a result.

If the Great Spirit intended that all animals and all humans should be perfect, then they would not be in your world, or even in mine. They would have achieved the summit of evolution, which is not possible because it is an eternal progression.

There is much to be done to end animal cruelty. There are wars constantly being fought between the forces of good and those of greed and selfishness, between the ones with knowledge and those who are ignorant. And there are the shortsighted people who do not realise the part animals play in your world and that they have as much right to be there as humans have. The battles will be fought, and gradually you will win.

"Will you say something about the next evolutionary stage

for birds and fish which are evolving in line with human beings? Is this the deva evolution? What is the next stage for insects, so many of which seem so far advanced and have a complicated 'civilisation' of their own?"

I do not think the word "civilisation" is correct. Applied to any life, civilisation is the means by which you adapt your societies and cultures.

If you ask will a bird ever become a human being, the answer is no.

The deva evolution is part of the elemental life that concerns fairies and similar aspects of being. They have their part to play in nature's growth. Evolution is part of the natural law for all life and is evidence that the Great Spirit is imbued with love. Evolution consists in growing from the lower to the higher all the time.

The law of evolution embraces every facet of life, the insect, the birds, the fish, the human. They all have their parts to play and are related to one another. No aspect of life is isolated; every form of life is integrated so that the totality forms a composite whole. You are part of the same law of evolution that is responsible for how animals progress.

If you work with the natural laws, if you are in harmony with them, you not only fulfil yourself, but at the same time you help the evolution of all other aspects of nature. The whole scheme is divinely ordered so that you play your parts as co-operative elements in it. Those who violate nature instead of working with it are performing a disservice to what they violate, and to themselves. Those who co-operate with nature are helping its growth and also helping the unfoldment of their spiritual natures.

"Does this mean that as human beings we have no special place but are part of the process?"

You are part of the eternal processes of life. Because you consider that man is a higher species than other forms of life, you have a responsibility to help what you regard as the lower, just as you desire that higher beings in our world should help you.

"Is there such a thing as a higher form of life in our world, so far as the animals are concerned?"

No, each animal has its own evolution to outwork. Whatever lives does so because it is spirit. Spirit is life, life is spirit. Therefore every living thing, creature, bird, fish, flower, tree, fruit, is spirit.

When you talk of higher and lower it is only a question of the stage of evolution that is reached as compared with other stages in the variegated forms of life. To the fish you may be a higher stage of evolution, but to the hierarchy of our world you are at a lower stage.

"We are making such slow progress to help animals. It seems to get worse and worse in this world."

This is the result of man being given a limited free will. If there were to be no problems, no struggles, no sacrifices, no difficulties, you could not evolve. Progress is achieved when you are confronted with difficulties, not when your life is easy. It is an inherent part of evolution that there has to be a "crucible" from which each soul must emerge as part of a testing time to ensure that it can call on latent strength.

Progress is slow in some aspects and faster in others. It is man's responsibility to ensure that he is at peace with all who share the earth with him. But whatever happens, there is compensation as part of the natural law.

You have the responsibility of ensuring that animals should evolve according to their path of evolution. If you abnegate your responsibility, then you must pay the price for it. Those who practise cruelty will have to pay the spiritual price for everything they do.

Alas, the innocent always suffer. We cannot thwart the operation of natural law. If a brutal man commits a murder he will have to pay the price, and there will be compensation for the victim. The law of compensation will always outwork itself. The Great Spirit has ensured that divine justice will be meted out to everybody through the laws of compensation and retribution.

"In nature it seems that the strongest survives. If that is right, how would this be applied to humans and spiritual matters?"

Have you heard of symbiosis? Isn't that a law of nature? And isn't it a fundamental law that the co-operation existing in nature enables nature to fulfil its purpose?

The tree absorbs the poisons in the atmosphere, purifies it, and enables you to be healthier. Is that strength, or is it not harmony and co-operation at work?

"I think of animals especially."

Which animals have survived from prehistoric times? The elephant. Was that a brute? It was not. The animal was a vegetarian that did not prey on other animals. All the others have not survived. Which is the strongest?

You have a garden. If you work with nature you get results. If you abuse nature, you don't get results. Show love not only to your fellow beings but to animals. Do not exploit people, do not exploit animals and do not exploit nature. Then you are helping not only the people of your world, but everything that exists to have that peace, orderliness and harmony that is the ultimate purpose of evolution, the law devised by the greatest power in the universe.

19: The Last Supper

Was it mere coincidence that thirteen – one of whom, born a Jew, began his main teaching mission at the age of 30 – gathered in an upper room?

We met to listen to wise counselling, and to break bread together. Though none on earth realised, Silver Birch had set the scene for his own Last Supper.

At their St John's Wood flat, Maurice and Sylvia Barbanell greeted earthly guests in the book-lined sitting-room. Its focal point is the fine portrait of Silver Birch painted by psychic artist Marcel Poncin.

Before the seance began, Maurice Barbanell balanced the sitters' positions with care to achieve the maximum polarity.

Then, in the glorious light of a warm summer evening – for Silver Birch had no need of darkness – the two-world communion began.

Always the circle started with the hymn, "Open My Eyes," and a prayer. Greetings were then exchanged between friends living in different planes of vibration. Earth-dwellers placed one hand on the small table inside the circle. As the "Good evenings" were uttered, and the spirit recipient's name pronounced, the table rocked. Sometimes gently, sometimes forcefully, each other-world visitor made his presence known.

The medium took his customary place on the low sofa beside his wife, and removed his thick-lensed spectacles. His easily recognisable, nasal voice bade his guests continue chatting.

Then he bowed his head. His eyes were to remain closed fast for the next ninety minutes.

The transformation began.

The room became alive with an indescribable upsurge of spirit power.

Suddenly, through the lips of the now entranced medium, came the familiar deep, guttural, heavily accented tones – the voice of Silver Birch.

Some have commented in surprise that the voice recorded on the cassette, "Silver Birch Speaks," resembles that of an old man, belying the guide's portrait which depicts a Red Indian in the prime of life.

On this night the spirit power, supplemented by that generated by the several mediums present, caused the voice to be strong and vigorous.

So the guide, using the physical body of his earthly instrument, spoke, fluently and calmly.

As always, he first dedicated a moving and beautiful invocation to the Great Spirit.

★ ★ ★

May the power of the Great White Spirit bless you all.

Let us follow our usual practice and put on one side any thought of fear, worry, anxiety or trouble.

Let us try to achieve the closest possible harmony with one another so that we become united in our desire to add to the wondrous knowledge we have received. Then let us aspire to the highest we can reach, the supreme power, the infinite creator of all life whose wisdom has devised the universe in which we dwell and the natural laws which control, regulate and sustain every facet of being, mighty or minute, so that none and nothing are excluded from the orbit of this overshadowing, presiding love.

We strive to draw as close as we can to that infinite storehouse of wisdom, truth and inspiration which has added to our understanding of who and what we are, what it is we have to achieve, the gifts to unfold so that we can play our part in shaping those processes of eternal creation and help others who are less fortunate than we are.

We welcome into our midst the evolved spiritual beings of the hierarchy whose one desire is to serve us, to enrich and help us to increase our receptivity so that we become even greater channels through whom the sublime power of the spirit will stream and bring its rich benefits to those who are unaware of it.

Our task is to heal the sick, to uplift the fallen, to give strength to the weary, to guide the ones who have lost their way and banish the superstition and error, and to flood your world with the great light of truth so that they may no longer dwell in the shadows.

We pray that we may be worthy of the power that seeks to use us in all these divine tasks. This is the prayer of Thy Indian servant who seeks always to serve.

★   ★   ★

Silver Birch first greeted a valued friend whose love for animals is legendary. She has spent a lifetime studying, filming and winning the trust of countless creatures all over the world.

Less well known are her superb natural gifts of healing and mediumship.

When she flew into London from her Kenya home to visit the circle, Silver Birch indicated his awareness of difficulties in her own development group.

It is very sad when those who have the knowledge do not behave in accordance with its implications.

We are aware of all human failings, and recognise that we are dealing with people imperfect like ourselves who still have much progress to make.

We cannot function where there is disharmony. The power of the spirit must of necessity work where there is unity of purpose, co-operation, concord and the desire to serve, to do what is best for others who are unaware of these great truths.

So if the time comes when you cannot achieve harmony, it is best to part.

The Great Spirit with infinite wisdom has bestowed on you the gifts of the spirit, which you must use. A way will be found for you to be able to dispense the healing and the comfort, the guidance which can help people in a land where the power of the spirit has very few bridges. You can recreate the bastion so that from there we can begin all over again. Lessons are to be learned. You will triumph because you have much work to do.

It was not by accident you were taken to the land where you dwell. Conditions are difficult at present. It is a kind of maelstrom but good will emerge.

★ ★ ★

Next Silver Birch welcomed a medium whose public work had spanned more than 40 years.

The Great Spirit with infinite wisdom conferred the gifts of the spirit on those who can utilise them in the service of others.

To this extent you have been richly blessed. You have been helped when no earthly power could have helped you. The power of the spirit has done so; it has fortified you, given you strength in weakness, provided succour when it was necessary.

You have never been left alone. Always that mighty power of love has surrounded you and provided you with all that is necessary for your sustenance. I know there have been times when you had to count the physical pennies to see whether there were enough. But those who serve are always served.

There is a plan, an overall plan, into which we all fit. We all have our work to do.

You have helped many to replace their tears of sorrow with the smile of certainty.

You have brought them knowledge when they thought it was unobtainable. You have enabled love to be reunited with its beloved. You have helped to heal the sick, provided guidance for those who thought there was no way to turn. You still have work to do. So do not worry. Have no fear.

I do not have to tell you that the ministers, the channels, the instruments of the Great Spirit must not expect to live in a bed of roses. That is not their way.

They have to meet with real difficulty and challenge, with the thorns and the stones on the pathway. They have to learn that the only real foundation is the power of the spirit. Nowhere on earth can they find this foundation which will provide them with the basis on which to build their lives.

You will not want. You will not go hungry. You will not go thirsty. We cannot promise that you will live in the lap of luxuries. That would not be good for you. All you require will be provided, the wherewithal will be available for you. Just continue to uplift those who come to you.

What you and other instruments of the spirit do is something that no other people, no other religion, no other movement, no other philosophy, no other science, no doctor, no economist can do.

You can point the way, show people the purpose of earthly life, how to develop so that the latent divinity finds a greater expression, how to possess the eternal riches of the spirit that never tarnish, that once gained can never be lost. That is your function.

Always rejoice when you can help a soul. If you cannot, it is not your fault. If people are not ready to be helped, there is nothing you can do. Just be available to give the unique service that you can perform. That is what we ask of you, and no more.

You promised to do this work even though you may not be aware of it. You are fulfilling yourself.

★ ★ ★

To an old friend, a woman journalist, Silver Birch gave these words of encouragement.

There is a power, there is a plan. I who have lived much longer than any of you can only marvel at its efficacy and the fact that it cannot fail.

When I see you looking worried I think to myself: "What are they worrying about? Everything is going to be quite all right."

Unless you had the darkness you could not appreciate the light, unless you had the depths you could not go to the heights.

Life must be a polarity. You must have what you consider is the good and what you consider the bad, but they are equal and opposite. They are also equal in the service they have to perform.

If you had eternal sunshine you would not appreciate it. It is because you have the rain and the clouds, the thunder and the lightning that you appreciate the sunshine when it comes.

Life is a polarity. Action and reaction, equal and opposite; they are the two sides of the same coin.

Hate can be translated into love, and unfortunately love can be translated into hate. It is the same power. It is only a question of the way it functions.

Every aspect can be used for good or for ill. That is the element of your choice, your free will, your decision, your judgement. That is the attribute the Great Spirit has conferred on you so that you are able to make the decisions and not merely be puppets or marionettes.

You have free will to make your decisions. We try to guide you as much as we can so that you make the right one. Sometimes we have to let you go your own way to learn lessons, but we know you will emerge unscathed and add to the store of your experience.

Your life is a polarity. You must have the challenges, and face obstacles and handicaps, otherwise that tremendous latent divinity within you will never find expression.

The greatest things in life are the ones that are the most difficult, otherwise they would not be the greatest. If the prizes of the spirit were easily attained they would not be worth while.

Welcome difficulty; do not be afraid of it. Turn it to your service so that you rise above it and allow the many unexpressed powers you possess to be able to show themselves.

You have a tremendous reservoir within yourselves that is seldom tapped, and certainly very infrequently utilised.

You have nothing to fear. There was a great soul in your world who was called to lead his country at a time of one of its greatest crises. He told the millions who listened to him, "You have nothing to fear but fear itself." Fear is the shadow; it is not the reality. Have no fear. Bask in the sunlight of knowledge.

When the journalist mentioned having regrets, the guide added:

It is good sometimes to shed tears to provide relief and to bring comfort as a result. It is better to shed tears than to have within you bottled up emotions which are unexpressed.

★ ★ ★

Next the guide greeted an outstanding healer whose gift has cured patients in many countries.

He was about to leave for a third healing mission to Canada, and was scheduled to appear on television. Silver Birch told him:

The only value of the past is that it is the pattern of the present and the future. It has lessons to teach. It is part of the tapestry of earthly life. All its threads play their part in forming a pattern which will emerge and show it is based on a unity and harmony of purpose.

Your gift is not only a privilege, but also a responsibility. You are the receptacle, the channel, the vessel, the instrument through which a divine power is transmitted.

It is a sacred power, the power of life itself, the power

that can perform what others regard as miracles and provide health where there is sickness and give hope where individuals fear there could be no hope for them.

There is a wondrous task to perform. Do the best you can. Always the way will be shown. There will be brought to you those whom you can help.

I said to you the last time you were here that you would not be able to help everyone. Some are not spiritually ready. In that case it is not your fault. They have had the opportunity; they have missed it. Shed a silent tear for them.

"I do the best I can."

That is all that is expected of you. We do the best we can. We have to work with conditions which are not of our choosing.

All we ask is your co-operation. All we offer is our co-operation. We will not dictate. We will not seek to compel. We will win you with love and reason by pointing out what it is you can achieve not only to serve others but to fulfil yourself.

What you do clergymen cannot do, ministers cannot do, rabbis cannot do, unless they possess similar powers. The Great Spirit, with wisdom that is often incomprehensible and seemingly mysterious to your world, bestows the gifts not on those who think they should possess them, but on those whom infinite wisdom decides should be their possessors.

You have work to do. Rejoice because of the opportunities provided.

"Recently I had two patients suffering from the same illness. One was completely cured. The other one did not respond to the healing. Why is this?"

Every happening has its purpose. There are no accidents or coincidences, only planned operations, laws of cause and effect at work.

At some stage in human life the Great Spirit provides his children with an opportunity not only of finding themselves, but of achieving self-realisation. To do so the soul has to be touched.

Now if the soul is not touched the power of the spirit cannot work. If a cure is achieved and a soul is not touched, then the healing has failed in its purpose also.

The whole object of our return is to demonstrate spiritual reality so that people will stop chasing shadows and learn what are the basic fundamental truths on which all life in its infinite varieties are based.

The power that streams through you was available to both. One responded, the other did not.

"It made me very sad."

Of course it is sad, but it is sad for them. You cannot cure them all. There are some who will never be cured in your world. They are paying karmic debts and have lessons to learn. Healing will not touch them. That is why I say to do the best you can. You are there to be available. What happens after you have done healing is not your responsibility. You have to provide the best conditions, to be the purest channel. Reach out to the highest you can attain; that is your responsibility. But remember you are helping souls to find themselves that otherwise would not have done so.

Just go forward. Welcome the task each day brings. Rejoice that you can continue to be the channel for the greatest power in the universe.

Silver Birch had given his medium's secretary a rare and

prized invitation to the home circle.

Seeking the guide's reassurance on a projected change within the newspaper which Maurice Barbanell edited, the visitor was told:

You will always be running into difficulties either sooner or later, but they will not be those which cannot be conquered. Have no fears. I am only a very small cog in a very large wheel. That wheel will turn because the power responsible is the greatest in the universe, the mightiest in the vast cosmos.

It is the power that brought into being the whole of your world, the universe, the planets, the stars, the oceans, the seas, the mountains, the flowers, the birds, the beasts, the humans.

That power will not fail you. We have not come back to your world to indulge in failure. We are here to stay. None will ever thwart the power of the spirit.

Place your confidence in us. We will not fail you. Sometimes we have been failed by those who should not have failed us, but that is an element which has to be taken into consideration.

The work will continue. We will not be turned away. We will not be scoffed out of existence. We are here to stay.

You are playing your part, as the hymn says, "You in your small corner and I in mine."

Have no fear. When I was asked to volunteer a long time ago to do this work, I was told it would not be easy; perhaps it would be the greatest challenge I have ever had to face. When the plan was explained to me I said, "I will do my best."

You see now the power of the spirit has spread all

over the world through the printed word. We have reached people.

All I had was one instrument, a willing instrument. I won the love and co-operation of many friends. I now have a countless number whose hearths and hearts provide me with the warmth that is so needed by us when venturing into your dark, cheerless, cold, wearisome, dismal world.

Why some prefer darkness when they could have light is something I do not understand.

The power that emanates from the Great Spirit will not be defeated. It may be delayed, it may be held up. It will not be overcome; we shall overcome.

I started with one instrument. Now we have many friends in your world in many lands. I rejoice at the opportunities that have been provided to help them when they thought no help was possible because they were in difficult conditions, isolated places surrounded by bigotry and intolerance. And so the power can spread the word of the spirit.

Now you have cassettes so we can reach these people. They realise that no matter where they are, the mighty power girdles the whole of your earth and can reach the children of the spirit wherever they may be.

We are here to stay in your world. We have tasks to perform. We still have to root out a lot of ignorance and still to demonstrate the supreme reality of the spirit.

This is the whole dynamic, this is the motivation, this is what your services are all about, the spirit at work reaching wherever it can and bringing within its radius souls who are unaware of the tremendous love, light and richness that this tremendous power has to offer.

There is no clergyman, no rabbi, no minister, no archbishop, no prelate, no pope who can do what you can do.

They can only repeat theological creeds, dogmas and doctrines. They cannot quicken and touch souls by demonstrating the spirit is the only permanent reality in life.

"Would you say in the olden days the prophets were the mediums of the times?"

Yes, of course.

"They were persecuted by the priests."

The priestcraft won and the prophets lost. But this time the prophets are winning and the priestcraft is losing. We will continue to infiltrate wherever we can so that when we are confronted with souls that are ready we can touch and help them so that they can develop their gifts to serve others. I am always grateful to do whatever I can to serve.

20: Who Is Silver Birch?

Silver Birch is not my name. It is the name of the Indian spirit I use as a transformer that enables me to lower my vibrations and reach your world. The name does not matter. I have not revealed the name I bore on earth because it has no value so far as I am concerned.

I am not a Red Indian. I belong to another race in another part of the world that goes back much further. I attained a certain stage in my spiritual evolution where it seemed there was no necessity for me to return to the confines of your world.

We have what could be called a hierarchy. These are evolved spiritual beings – masters, if you like. Their task is to ensure the harmonious working of plans that have been made.

I was asked if I would forfeit what I have earned through evolution, and return as close as I could come to your world and act as a messenger for these evolved beings. My function would be to transmit their teachings so that those who were ready would be able to realise what we have to offer.

I agreed to do so, and that is the mission on which I have been engaged for a long time.

I had to learn your English language. It is not a language which I spoke when I was on earth. I was told when I embarked on my mission that I would have to familiarise myself with the language you use, its grammar and its syntax.

There was a problem, because I required a medium to make contact with your world. I could not reach it myself, because the stage of evolution I had reached was of a different vibration and not suitable for that purpose. I had to have what you call a transformer.

They found for me the spirit body of a Red Indian that was suitable to be my medium for transmitting the teachings which are given to me to impart.

I am not going to tell you that the Red Indian civilisation, which if I may say so was superior to the white one, was free from all imperfections or cruelties. But to a large extent the blame must be laid at the door of the "superior" whites who introduced the iniquities of the white one.

There are no perfect beings. If you were perfect, you would not be where you are now.

The Red Indians made their contribution. Their ethics and morals were high. They had their appreciation of nature, an understanding of the spiritual laws, the desire to achieve brotherhood among themselves; but they had their faults.

They were masters of psychic laws, and understood their operation. They also had a greater knowledge of spiritual laws. Like everybody else who comes to our world, they were confronted with the law of cause and effect. They received compensation or made retribution for whatever had happened in earthly life.

There is no exemption from the operation of natural law. Every race, every nation and every culture has its contribution to make in your world. It is like a mighty orchestra in which every instrument contributes its part to achieve the harmony of music which produces the greatest beauty.

What are considered the uncivilised and the lowliest have their parts to play in the great unfolding scheme. But whoever they are and wherever they may be, they are all spiritual beings. The essence of divinity runs through all of them and makes them one in a common family of the Great Spirit. Differences of colour, language, race and nationality are infinitesimal compared with the spiritual unity which is their fundamental basis.

I am not an infallible spirit teacher who never makes mistakes and has achieved the summit of progress. That cannot be so, because progress is eternal. There is no period to perfection, because the more you achieve the more you realise there is to be achieved.

The great value of what we have to offer is a sublime truth from the storehouse of divine wisdom and inspiration. We never ask you to take us on trust. We do not say that you must do what we suggest. Nor do we insist that there are no other ways by which you can obtain a greater attunement with the Great Spirit.

What we do affirm, and with all the strength at our command, is that the truths of the spirit can be tested by your reason, intelligence, and experience. There is no threat of punishment if you say we have told you things which you do not accept.

The Great Spirit has endowed you with a measure of free will. You are not puppets. You have intelligence, reason, the ability to judge, to decide, to reflect, to form your own opinions and to be guided by the experiences that come your way.

Our desire is to win you and your co-operation through the assent of your reason. We do not want to offend it, because it is one of the gifts the Great Spirit has bestowed.

You have your work to do, your parts to play. Life is always a polarity. If there were no darkness there would be no light. If there were no trouble there could never be any peace. If the sun always shone you would not appreciate it.

You have to learn sometimes through conditions that seem a nuisance. When you come to my world you will look back and say, "We learned our best lessons not when the sun was shining, but when the storm was at its greatest, when the thunder roared, the lightning flashed, the clouds obscured the sun and all seemed dark and hopeless."

It is only when the soul is in adversity that some of its greatest possibilities can be realised. You will not attain spiritual mastery in six easy lessons. It is a difficult path to tread. And as you tread it the familiar signposts and landmarks are left behind. But the more you progress, the more you achieve an inner confidence based on what you have earned for yourself.

Forget the past. It is behind you; what is in front of you is more important.

Naturally the past was responsible for the causes producing the effects which you are now experiencing, but you are producing the causes that in turn will produce the effects. Try to sow the right seeds, which is a platitude but still true. Have no fear; fear is the child of ignorance. Live in the light of knowledge.

Your earthly lives will provide you with many

opportunities to serve others as you have been served. The way will always be found.

You are human, you will make mistakes; you are fallible, you will err. You are weak, because human nature is not all strength. The very essence of humanity is that it has its defects; that is why you are on earth.

You will not achieve perfection in your world, but you will learn the lessons that it has to offer so that spiritually you become more equipped for that world which you will inhabit one day.

★　★　★

Silver Birch always refuses thanks.
He explained to two first-time visitors:

I insist on this because I deprecate very strongly an aspect I have seen too often. It is known as guide worship, and we do not desire worship.

The only power which is to be worshipped is the Great Spirit, the infinite spirit, the supreme creator, the acme of all light, love, wisdom, truth and inspiration.

We do not want to defer any worship from where it should be sent.

I am not the possessor of all knowledge. I have not reached the end of my spiritual progress. There is still a long way for me to go. But I have, because of a longer experience, been able to acquire some truths that have enriched my life.

I have retraced my steps to share what I have learned with those who are ready to receive it. I am not perfect. I am still human and fallible. I can make mistakes. But I will always do the best I can to help those I can reach with the truths I enunciate, which are given to me.

It is my privilege to serve. I am fortunate to be able to

express what others tell me to say, and they are the ones who matter. These are the masters, the hierarchy, the ones who are charged with the task of seeing that the divine plan will be fulfilled. If I help any one soul to find the light, I rejoice.

★   ★   ★

The guide was asked, "Do you ever anticipate coming back to incarnate on this earth?"

No, I am not coming back. I have served my apprenticeship in your world. I only return to help you and others, and remind you of those eternal truths and laws which cannot fail. I try to cheer you, and remind you that you are spiritual beings living in a transient world as far as you are concerned. You are privileged to have had the reality revealed to you. Be grateful for what has been shown and has changed the whole tenor of your lives.

I am richly blessed to have found in your world so many friends who are able to accept the teachings I am privileged to expound and which are given to me from higher stages of being. I know that they contain within themselves divine truths which can be helpful to many. The problem is that people must be ready to receive them.

★   ★   ★

A medium who complained of loneliness was surprised when Silver Birch remarked:

I experience far more loneliness than you do.

I do not belong to the sphere which I have to inhabit to do this work. My place is somewhere else, where the conditions are far more favourable, where my associates and colleagues are radiant beings. I see them and meet them only when I withdraw from your world and take counsel with them and others who help me. Your world is a most unattractive place to us.

We are familiar with a richness, grandeur and nobility of living such as can be enjoyed by all who have evolved to the stage where they are aware of what life fundamentally has to offer.

I come back to your world with its vibrations of hate, greed and stupidity. I warm myself against this desolate coldness at the hearths of those who are my friends and extend love to me. And thus it makes it all worth while.

I regard myself as very fortunate that I have been able to make so many friends in your world. All I have to offer is what I regard as fundamental truths which are conveyed to me and clothed in your language so that they can be accepted by those who are ready to receive them.

There is nothing we have to say that will insult your intelligence or make your reason revolt. We have only love to offer you, for love is the coin of the spirit. To serve is noble. There is no higher or greater religion than service.

A journalist asked whether the time had arrived for Silver Birch to reveal his identity. The guide replied:

I am who I am. My name is not important. What is important is that we can help people. I regard it as a great privilege that I have been able to serve, and that I have made so many friends in your world.

I too have had to meet challenges and difficulties, but I welcomed them because I knew that, with the power that is behind us, we must and will prevail.

You are in a position where you can help people. It is a unique service that you can render, more than the churches, the synagogues, the chapels, the scientists and economists. More than any of these, you have the priceless boon of being channels for the sublime power of the spirit, the greatest force in the universe, the power that emanates from the Great Spirit of all life, for without it there is nothing. It is spirit that endowed life with all its many countless manifestations. Rejoice at the opportunity to serve.

The guide made these comments at the last sitting before Christmas:

As you know, this is the time when temporarily I say farewell to earth and return to those inner spheres which are more my natural home. It is a sad moment for me because I will miss the opportunities of being with you. But it is essential that I should receive the refreshment that cannot be obtained where I now am, in order that my spiritual batteries are recharged for the tasks that are still to be done.

I will find out how I have fared, whether I have acquitted myself as I should have done. What I do know is that I have earned the love of many more. This of course is a great measure of comfort for me.

Hold your heads high; do not let them get bowed down. The power of the spirit will not desert you. My voice will be silent for a while, but my love will remain with you. When we meet again, after you have started what is a new year in your accounting of time, we will resume the solemn tasks on which we are engaged.

Let us all strive to attune ourselves to the highest that we can reach. Let us try as much as we can to be increasingly aware of what the Great Spirit has to offer His children, immeasurable love and power, and abiding inner peace. May the Great Spirit bless you all.

21: Maurice Barbanell's Own Story

Maurice Barbanell, always a keen journalist, prepared his own obituary.

Who could better tell this fascinating story?

It also affords the reader the opportunity to compare his writing style with that of Silver Birch.

★   ★   ★

I have been told that my psychic story really begins in a previous incarnation of which I have no knowledge.

Red Cloud, the guide of Estelle Roberts, who gave me my finest evidence of individual Survival after death, and in whose seance room "Psychic News" was born, said I had made a promise in a former existence. This was to reincarnate and devote my life to spreading Spiritualism.

So far as I am aware my psychic story started undramatically at a meeting of the Ghetto Social and Literary Club in London's East End. I was the unpaid secretary with a twofold task.

It was my job to obtain, without fee, famous literary and artistic figures to speak on a variety of subjects, a feat I achieved with success. This was mostly because these eminent authors were intrigued to find cultural yearnings in London's darkest East End.

My other task was, irrespective of what the speaker said, to lead the opposition so as to ensure a good discussion. My colleagues always told me that I managed to excel in this direction.

During my secretaryship some friends invited me to be present at a seance, the first I had ever attended.

Only when it ended did they tell me it was a mock affair staged for fun. Nevertheless, as a teenager it produced subconsciously an antagonism to Spiritualism.

Like so many young men I had abandoned orthodox religion. My mother was devoutly religious. My father was an atheist who steadfastly refused to accompany her to any orthodox services despite her lament that his absence would shock their friends.

In my youth I heard so many arguments about religion between my parents, in which incidentally my father always won, that I adopted his atheism, which later changed to agnosticism.

It is necessary to mention this personal background to set the scene for what followed.

One night at our social and literary club there was no eminent speaker. Instead our guest was a young man named Henry Sanders, who spoke about his experiences in Spiritualism. When he finished my colleagues turned to me for my usual opposing opening speech from the floor.

I surprised them. Despite my then fairly recent mock seance attendance, I said this was a subject on which only those with experience could venture any worthwhile opinions. As I had made no personal investigation my opinions were, therefore, valueless. Naturally the rest of the evening was not a hectic one for discussion.

When it was over Sanders approached me. Was I serious, he asked, in my statement that only those with experience based on inquiry should venture to declare their views? If so, was I prepared to investigate?

"Yes," I replied. Moreover I would reach no conclusion until I had spent six months on this quest. I still have the diary in which I noted the date when the six months would end. Here I am, a half a century later, still inquiring . . .

Sanders invited me to attend a home circle which met in a nearby tenement. The date was arranged. I went accompanied by Sylvia, who was then my fiancée and now my wife. The circle in this dingy block was composed of a mixture of young and old Jews who all seemed earnest though unprepossessing.

The medium, a middle-aged woman, Mrs Blaustein, was said to go into trance. In that state, I was told, entities belonging to differing nationalities would control and speak through her.

This happened, but did not impress me. So far as I could tell, there was no evidence which would satisfy me that these indeed were "dead" foreigners speaking through her lips.

Nevertheless in view of my promise I presented myself at the second sitting where a similar demonstration by her was given. It seemed to me that at one stage of the proceedings I fell asleep, either through boredom or being tired. When I woke I apologised. I was told to my surprise, "You have been a Red Indian."

It was my first mediumistic trance, but what happened was a complete blank to me. Nevertheless the guide known as Silver Birch had broken formidable earth barriers and spoke a few words in a husky and almost guttural voice. It is far different from what I am assured are the simple but eloquent tones that so many have now heard.

The sequel was the formation of my own home circle where the Silver Birch entity gradually developed as his control became a seemingly simple process of merging his individuality with mine. There were degrees of awareness in this unfolding process of my mediumistic development. I was not keen on the trance condition, probably through my vanity in wanting to know what was said and done through my bodily mechanism.

At one stage there was a fascinating happening. As I lay in bed on the night after sitting, everything that had been said through me unrolled on a kind of cinema screen so that I became familiar with all that the others had heard.

This no longer obtains because of the intervention of Hannen Swaffer, the famous journalist, whom I came to know intimately. Our association began when we spent three years addressing public meetings all over Britain, to audiences totalling 250,000, at weekends. Sometimes there were two and even three meetings on one day.

Always we travelled by car from London on the Saturday morning; often we returned in the early hours of Monday. The meetings had to be held at weekends because of my commercial life, which virtually ended when "Psychic News" was launched in 1932. Then my association with Swaff took another form.

He was intrigued by my trance mediumship and came to love Silver Birch. Swaff said the guide's teachings were being wasted as they were heard only by a handful of people. As a natural propagandist he wanted them to be disseminated, reaching the largest possible number of people, and thought the perfect vehicle was "Psychic News."

I demurred. Obviously, I said, I would be open to criticism by publicising my own mediumship in the newspaper I edited. Finally, after much argument, I agreed to do so, provided my identity was withheld.

There was another problem to be solved. The guide was then known, as he still is to a few intimates, by a nickname which was deemed unsuitable for publication. He was asked to choose one for this purpose. Silver Birch was his selection.

The next morning, in my office, the mail included a postcard from Scotland with no name or address of the sender, but with a splendid photograph of Silver Birch trees on it.

The teachings of what was called, as it still is, Hannen Swaffer's home circle regularly appeared in "Psychic News." Curiosity was constantly aroused as to the medium's identity which for long was kept secret.

Swaff, however, brought so many visitors from among his famous friends that I felt the stage was reached when the mystery should be ended. I wrote an article announcing that I was Silver Birch's medium.

I should mention in passing that, when you work in a confectionery factory, you soon lose your taste for sweets. And when you are an editor you are not attracted by publicity as too many humans are.

The Silver Birch teachings have been recorded by two shorthand writers. The first was Billy Austen, then my assistant editor. His place was taken by Frances Moore, who still acts as "the scribe," the name by which the guide always calls her.

Occasionally the seances have been tape-recorded. There are several of these recordings obtainable today. Once even a gramophone record was made for public sale.

Because all the sessions were being reported in shorthand, I was asked if I would forego the practice of having the proceedings recalled for me later in bed. It was explained that an expenditure of psychic power became involved. I agreed.

To test the state of trance Silver Birch once asked Swaff to stick pins into me. Though blood was drawn I felt nothing.

There are critics calling themselves psychic researchers who dismiss guides as the medium's secondary personalities. I am aware of all the problems involved in trance mediumship.

Mainly they stem from the fact that a guide has to control the medium's subconscious mind.

This, unlike a telephone, is a living thing and, therefore, is bound to colour to some extent whatever is transmitted from the spirit world. Development consists in obtaining mastery over the subconscious mind.

In my working life I use words every day. I have never yet written or dictated an article with which I was satisfied when I read it. Inevitably I find, when looking at the typed material, that I can improve it by altering words, phrases and sentences.

No such problem arises with the guide's teachings. These flow perfectly, requiring usually only commas, semi-colons or full stops. Another interesting aspect is the occasional use of words that I regard as archaic and do not form part of my normal vocabulary.

Silver Birch's distinctive and separate individuality – I believe there is a spiritual relationship – has been proved to me and to my wife many times. In the early days we had what was probably our most remarkable evidence.

He told Sylvia that in connection with a certain matter which presented a seemingly insoluble problem to us both, he would provide an answer. At the time we both attended the regular direct voice sittings of Estelle Roberts. Silver Birch said at the next one he would speak through the trumpet to Sylvia and mentioned the words he would say.

Of course Estelle was told nothing about this. You can imagine how curious we were to see what would happen. Estelle's guide, Red Cloud, was obviously in the picture because of the references he made that only Sylvia and I understood.

As the perfect master of spirit ceremonies he staged the matter admirably by keeping us waiting almost to the end. Then he said to Sylvia that the next communicator was for her. In the darkness on which Red Cloud always insisted, the phosphorescent trumpet moved towards her. Through it spoke Silver Birch and repeated the words he had promised to pronounce.

Evidence of separate identity came frequently in another circle where I sat regularly. Here with a non-professional medium named Nena Mayer we always had the direct voice. It was fascinating for me after

Silver Birch had spoken through me in trance to hear him communicating through the trumpet.

There are other occasions I could mention, but one more will suffice. A Fleet Street editor was bereaved when his son was killed in the last war. Without mentioning his name I asked Estelle whether he could be invited to a voice seance.

She replied by reminding me that the rule was that only those whom Red Cloud had agreed should be there could come. I said I would leave it and ask him when next we met.

The following day she telephoned me to say that Silver Birch had appeared to her and pleaded for my friend to be invited. So she agreed. Needless to say the "dead" son communicated to him and to his wife.

22: Silver Birch's Last Words

We end where we began. We began with the Power that has neither beginning nor ending, the power of the infinite spirit, the supreme creator, the apex of all being, the perfect love and wisdom.

You have been in the presence of liberated beings who have cast their radiance on us.

The ground on which we meet is hallowed and sacred because of the divine love that is manifested here.

Let us try wherever we can to be aware of this sublime, majestic power that is all around us. The mantle of divine love is wrapped around us.

Let us strive to make the will of the Great Spirit our will and earn that inner peace, serenity and tranquillity that comes to all those who attempt to be in unison with the Great Spirit of all life.

May the Great Spirit bless you all.